Hirst
Recollections of an Ashington Community

by Mike Kirkup

In the 1890s, the railway station could only be approached by opening a large wooden gate that stood next to the Portland Printing Works shop at the top of Station Bank. There were no shops at all on the other side of the road.

Previous page: A Peace Tea in 1919 between the front gardens of Chestnut Street.

First published in 2003 by

The People's History Ltd
Suite 1
Byron House
Seaham Grange Business Park
Seaham
Co. Durham
SR7 0PY

ISBN 1 902527 49 6

Contents

Acknowledgments

I would like to thank all those people who provided their own points of view of what the Hirst means to them, especially Allan Brownrigg, Ray Wear, Norman Hadland, Jim Main, Maurice Hook, Malcolm Mackenzie, Colin Wanless and Diane Green. And to John Mordue for access to his newspaper scrapbooks. I am also grateful to the many folks who loaned photos to add flavour to the text, such as Neil Taylor, Jack Wallace, John Murray, Norman Barron, Colin Furness, Ian S. Carr, Julian Trevelyan and Reuben Daglish, plus many many more. Thanks also to illustrator Vera Hook and artists from the *Ashington Colliery Magazine*.

Now 93 years old and still working from his studio in Maldon, Essex, Humphrey Spender is one of Britain's most revered and widely acclaimed photo-journalists. He visited Ashington around 1938 as part of a Mass-Observation group who were interested in documenting the life and culture of the mining community. Humphrey took many photos in and around the Hirst, and we are privileged to include two of them: on pages 41 and 113.

Scholarship boys from Hirst South School, 1934. Top left Dickie Slaughter became a first class piano accompanist, then Alan Proud who was destined to be manager of the Midland Bank on Station Bridge. Bottom left a lad called Atkinson, then John Foster who worked at the Welwyn before moving to Berkshire. Bottom right Ernie Richardson whose family lived in Sycamore Street.

Introduction

Lying sixteen miles north of Newcastle, Hirst, at the beginning of the 19th century, was sparsely populated, consisting of only a handful of farms and farm cottages. The word Hirst is taken from the Olde English *hyrste*, meaning a copse or wood.

Ashington and part of Hurst (1821 spelling) were in the Parish of Bothal in the year 1821. The remainder of Hurst was in Woodhorn Parish. The first recorded mention of 'Hurst' is in the *Memoirs of the Missionary Priests of the Roman Church* when it was stated: 'George Errington, gent, born at Hurst, Northumberland, was put to death at York on the 29th November 1536 for trying to convert a Protestant.'

At the east end of what is now known as Woodhorn Road, stood a farmhouse (above) with fortified battlements and a tower. This became known as 'Hirst Castle', standing at the top of the now familiar Castle Terrace. Stone dykes surrounded the building as protection against cattle raiders and other would-be marauders. Rumours that an underground passage led all the way to Bothal Castle were never verified.

Young Sam Snow arrived by train in Ashington in April 1894. He said: 'As I passed the railway line by the path to Woodhorn Village, I saw a group of men laying down the rail points and making ready for the sidings at Woodhorn Colliery. The railway station then was called 'Hirst'. On the east side of the railway station there was Nixon's Farm buildings with their cart sheds open to the roadside (now Wetherspoons pub) and two hinds' cottages where the shops now stand, opposite the Grand Corner.

'Very soon Hirst was alive with house building. With the erection of the Grand Hotel (*circa* 1894) the first block of Myrtle went up. A building contractor from Stakeford, called Gordon, began to build Chestnut Street. Poplar and Maple were commenced and, as houses increased, vans of domestic furniture could be seen daily, coming and going from the *Eldorado* of mining. Houses were going up like mushrooms.'

Miners came into the area from all over the UK as tin mines and lead mines became worked out and from Ireland to escape the potato famine. By 1900 the population had grown to over 7,000. But because of the introduction of two new pits at Woodhorn and Linton, the Hirst's population of 15,600 soon outstripped that of Ashington by over 8,000. This breakneck migration meant that finding a house became a nightmare.

The back streets between the Hirst colliery rows soon became mud baths (like the one seen here at Longhirst Colliery). Children were prone to pick up diseases such as diphtheria, enteric fever and typhoid while playing outdoors among open drains next to primitive privies. There was now an urgent need for the provision of a large recreational area in Hirst that would give the residents a place where they could relax and the children could let off steam while the adults played a game of bowls or tennis, or simply relax in pleasant surroundings away from the grime of the backstreets.

Many families arriving in the Hirst came from Scotland and Wales, others from Yorkshire, Lancashire and Cumberland. Of those who came from Durham and other parts of Northumberland, many were migrants from farther afield, still searching for somewhere to put down roots. By the 1920s, nearly all the Hirst children spoke with a broad Northumbrian accent, but many of their parents spoke with an alien tongue. These 'immigrants' were not absorbed into the Hirst of the early 1900s, but rather swamped the old village and established a new town of cosmopolitan Geordies. Hirst's population was growing, and growing quickly, but the streets remained huddled together with barely any breathing space.

HIRST IN THE EARLY DAYS

The first Stakeford Bridge was opened in 1909.

Towards the end of the 19th century the only way pedestrians or horses and carts could enter the area known as Hirst was to cross the River Wansbeck, near Black Close, either by walking across at low tide or by being hauled across on a ferry. There was a road access into Ashington, but that was two miles away at Sheepwash.

An enormous storm in the 1880s washed away part of Sheepwash Bridge, leaving the people of Ashington and Hirst virtually cut off from their near neighbours in Bedlington. This caused great hardship because the locals relied upon Cramlington Co-op for most of their groceries. This was before Ashington and Hirst had been allowed (by the Duke of Portland) to have their own Co-operative Society.

A group of men – some miners, some businessmen – got together and decided that what was needed was another bridge, based at Stakeford, which could be accessed until the Sheepwash Bridge was repaired. This new bridge was completed in 1909 and immediately opened up all manner of commerce with Hirst. Even after Sheepwash Bridge was repaired, the new bridge soon became more heavily used.

In 1910 Ashington Council, as part of its reorganisation plan, recognised the need for an open space at Hirst which could be used for recreation and play. It was then that work began on what we now know as Hirst Park. It took about five years to complete. This was how the *Morpeth Herald* reported the grand opening in September 1915:

Opening Ceremony At Hirst Park
Presentation Key to Councillor James Strong

The New Park at Hirst provided by the Ashington Urban District Council was opened on Saturday afternoon 25th September 1915 in the presence of a large and interested gathering. It is four years since the commencement was made with the Park, and it is hardly necessary to state that the completion of the pleasure grounds, as they are called, has been eagerly awaited.

AHN.18F.   HIRST PARK. ASHINGTON.

This was the Park-keeper's house.

The opening ceremony was performed by Cllr James Strong JP, chairman of the Parks Committee, who was made the recipient of a silver key, suitably inscribed, by his fellow councillors in honour of the occasion. In front of the main entrance to the Park, an improvised platform was erected. Cllr W.S. Pattison, chairman of the Council, presided. He was supported by Cllrs W. Wilson (retailer), Russell Cook (a prominent Ashington businessman), James Harwood, Robert (Bobby) Gray (an auctioneer who became a JP), Mr Joseph Bell, and Mr George Beaty (surveyor to the Council).

HIRST PARK, ASHINGTON.

Chairman's Remarks

Cllr W.S. Pattison said:

'I am glad to see so many people present to celebrate what is to this district a very important event. We have been waiting now for four years for this occasion, and when you entered the Park I feel sure your verdict is that it has been worthwhile.

'As a district we have now become one (Hirst with Ashington) but there is still rivalry because at the east end (Hirst) they are now better off, so far as a Park is concerned, than the people at the west end.'

It has not been established why, but in the early 1920s the playing field at Hirst Park was allowed to fall into a state of neglect (there had been a miners' strike in 1921). The children's playground facilities were taken down and the Park itself became a dumping ground for ashes from people's coal fires. During the 1926 General Strike that led to a six-month lock-out of miners, many families were evicted from their colliery houses and took refuge in the Hirst Park (playing area).

Agnes Mason was then a young girl of eight. She recalls: 'I was walking past the Hirst Park – it wasn't a park then, more like a rubbish dump – and I was amazed when I saw these tents which had been erected. It was like a tented village. Whole families were living there; clothes were hanging from washing lines; open fires were burning and women cooking meals; children were crying. It was awful.'

This is an aerial view of the Park around 1930 showing clouds of ash rising from the ground.

It was that same year (1926) that Ashington Coal Company thought they would find work to keep their employees busy. A new football pitch was needed at Hirst Welfare so the ACC asked dozens of locked-out miners if they would lead ash from Hirst Park to the Welfare to provide a base for a football pitch. Amazingly, men turned up in droves and did this work for nothing, leading many tons of ash on carts and in wheelbarrows the few hundred yards up to Hirst Welfare. This is how this vast operation was reported in the July 1926 edition of the *Ashington Colliery Magazine*:

'The centre football pitch on the Hirst Ground has been covered with a substantial layer of ashes to the extent of some 3,000 cartloads, and covered with turf, the result being a beautifully green and level football pitch. And it was all done in six weeks. It was a big job and a stiff one, involving on the part of the workers really hard work and not a little discomfort. For instance, those who filled steaming hot ashes into the carts at the ash heap in Hirst Park had to put in some arduous work in poor conditions. The work was undertaken for the benefit of the members of the Welfare Club in general. It was a work of service and we congratulate and thank them all.'

The inaugural match on the new pitch at Hirst Welfare was in August 1926. The top photo shows the Hirst Ex-Juniors and underneath is a shot of Freddie Booth OBE kicking off the match. Lower photo shows the Welfare Albion. The Ex-Juniors won this Knock Out Competition by 5-3. It was reported for the victors that 'Sep Miller led the attack with dash and determination'. Also singled out for praise were the 'dour Robson Brothers who ruthlessly nipped in the bud any attempt at finesse by the opposition'.

Winning the Booth Cup became a priority for all the teams in the Ashington Welfare League and many good squads won the coveted piece of silverware, such as Hirst East End in the early 1960s, with Jim Slaughter and Ernie Charlton on the committee. The Subsdiary Cup, introduced in the 1950s, was not as highly prized and was almost like a second-best trophy. It is believed the original Booth Cup now stands in the Northern Club trophy cabinet.

In this photo they might look like old men, but were only in their late teens. These five young pit lads had little to smile about in June 1926 – they were in the middle of a six-month miners' dispute that saw them 'locked out' of their jobs. Larry Kirkup, second left, and his friends are seen at the north side of the Park, entering from the playing field. You can spot the frame of the children's swings in the background.

Because of the stoppage, miners were obviously losing out on their pay packets. But others suffered too, including Ashington Hospital which relied on income from a levy on miners' pay to help in the day-to-day running of this comparatively new hospital, opened barely ten years. Consequently, the hospital lost out on a complete year's income. To compensate this, someone came up with the idea of having a 1927 Carnival Week to help raise some much-needed cash for the hospital. This took place in early September. Again, we quote the *Ashington Colliery Magazine* of October 1927: 'On Saturday 10th September, came the carnival finale. In spite of the rather depressing times, Ashington let itself go and turned out en masse.'

A huge procession was planned for the last day, and it was to form up on the field at Hirst Park. Harry Speight's father decided to enter the fancy dress parade with his dog 'Romo' dressed like an elephant, complete with howda and a collecting tin on its back. This is how the young Harry remembered that day: 'We had to meet at Hirst Park, and when we arrived everybody was getting ready to move off. The Park was filled with lorries and there were bands on top of a lot of them. There were at least three Salvation Army bands, and they were

surrounded by all kind of free gifts that were to be thrown out in the procession up the main street. Nearly all the lorries in the field were stacked with bottles of pop and goodies to hand out on the great March. The members of Ashington Operatic Society decked a lorry out like a pirate ship for the carnival (above).

'I was reet glad I was with my Ma and Da 'cos there was a big cannibal chasing some laddies over the Park with a greet nasty spear. I was frightened of him and stood between my Da and Romo until he moved away. Suddenly we heard a big drum split the afternoon air as the first band broke out the Hirst Park and made off up to Hawthorn Road, followed by lots of fancy dress people behind. And there was folks singing and dancing as they made their way out after the first band. And there were lots of Jazz Bands, too, mebbes four or five.'

The first colliery at Ashington was named after the Duke of Portland who lived in Bothal Castle, seen here – the pit's nickname was the Fell 'em Doon. Bothal Village was always a favourite walk on a Sunday afternoon for Hirst families.

The Grand Hotel was built in the 1890s. It soon became the focal point of the town and people from the Hirst would arrange rendezvous there with their friends, saying: 'Aa'll meet ye at the Grand Corner.'

Woodhorn Road looking towards Hawthorn Road at the turn of the 20th century.

PAVILION, HIRST, ASHINGTON.

The Pavilion Theatre was a venue for 'live' performances right up till the start of the Second World War. Gracie Fields sang there and so did George Formby. You can spot the narrow gauge railtrack on the left that was used for leading coal, with Sycamore Street in the background. The gang of boys were probably from the Hirst North School, attending around 1910.

Blacklock ... made the Shop too Posh
by Winnie Oxnard

After leaving school (1920s) I began to work for Blacklock's on Station Road. It was the tallest shop in Ashington with a basement and four floors. On the flat roof was a ballroom and tea garden with waitress service. They had mannequin parades, whist drives and a Tea-dance every Saturday afternoon. Both my sisters were working there when I started. The eldest was on Display, dressing the windows; the second left to go to Snow's, across the road.

But Robert Blacklock who lived at the Haven in Newbiggin made the shop too posh for Ashington. It wasn't the kind of place where a miner's wife could feel comfortable. The customers thought it was making too much money, the way the shop always sold the best clothes. But Blacklock's did have better merchandise than anyone else in town.

My father, who was a builder, helped to cover the upper front of the building with the white marmola exterior (still there). When it was finished it was a lovely store. Russell Cook's was nice, though not half as classy as Blacklock's (as seen in photo). But they kept the wages very low. I was only getting five shillings a week at fourteen years of age, which hardly kept me going in stockings.

But they mustn't have been making a profit and went into liquidation. A Bishop Auckland firm, Doggart's, took them over – they were Quakers. Many of the staff were finished, but some, including me, were kept on. I must have been lucky for jobs were hard to get in those days. However, I didn't stay long after that and followed my sister Doris across the road to Snow's. George Snow was a lovely man to work for. He would walk down the main street and see silk stockings on sale at McDonald's for one shilling a pair, and hurry into his own shop and tell me to mark ours down to elevenpence ha'penny. He sold cheaply but turned his stock over very fast. We sold everything there; I can remember selling motley-coloured Long Johns at one shilling a pair, and as the sizes went up you added thruppence to the price.

There's never been shops in Ashington like Blacklock's, Snow's or Russell Cook's (seen above on left of Grand Corner) since they closed. You knew that you were buying quality then, but now ... well, it's not the same.

By the 1920s Woodhorn Road was beginning to take shape.

United Bus Company

The familiar livery of United was first seen on the streets of Hirst in 1920, but the Lowestoft-based firm had been in existence since 1912 when it began operations simultaneously in Sussex and Durham. In 1919 the company purchased a number of War Department ambulances and converted them into passenger vehicles at their bodywork depot in Lowestoft. It was then they moved into Northumberland. Initially there was no bus station in Ashington, and the buses picked up passengers from bus stops dotted along Station Road (as seen in photo). United built a garage in 1920 and in 1936 eventually opened a depot and terminus on the site of what was Hirst Farm, later Nixon's, then Dungait's Farm.

In time there was a bus stop at practically every corner end down Milburn Road. This had been known as the New Road when the streets of Clyde and Severn were being built in the 1890s; Hirst already had an 'Aad' (Old) Road, now called North Seaton Road. The New Road became so busy with buses coming along almost every five minutes bound for Newbiggin, Newcastle or Blyth, that it became a death trap and numerous accidents occurred. Ashington Council decided to slash the long gardens at the bottom of the road to make it wider and safer. It was renamed 'Milburn' after one of the coal barons who also owned Milburn Estates, a company that had bought up most of the land east of the railway line. Here you see an early example of a United bus.

This wooden railway bridge was built over the River Wansbeck in the 1850s. A link on the Blyth and Tyne Railway came to the area in 1872 when stations were opened at North Seaton and Newbiggin. It was planned initially to take the track in a straight line from North Seaton to the seaside, but the vicar of St John's, Seaton Hirst Church, refused to allow the rail company wayleave through the church's land. So to reach Newbiggin, a loop was made to the north of Ashington. A few years later a station was built and named Hirst Station, but the Ashington Coal Company soon objected to this name, giving the reason that there were too many Hirsts in existence in England and that mistakes might be made. Being heavily represented on Ashington Council when it was formed in 1896, the ACC, as in most things, got its own way and it was re-named Ashington Railway Station. Hirst had lost out again.

Early Transport
by Florence Buck

The London and North Eastern Railway used to have the monopoly of passengers travelling from Ashington to the north, west and south. The fares charged then (pre-1920) were exorbitant – 5 shillings return to Newcastle. Around 1921, the United Bus Company first encroached upon the territory of the railway. United bought 20 reconditioned Army ambulances and parked them in a field (Dungait's Farm) as they had no garage then. The buses charged one shilling and ninepence return to Newcastle and, naturally, the railway lost most of its custom.

As the United Bus Company became greater, the owners (based in Lowestoft) built a huge garage at the bottom of Lintonville Terrace where they now (1931) garage the most up-to-date omnibuses. In 1930 the LNER and United decided it was useless to hold out against each other and formed one single company. The United Bus Company changed the colour of their buses to suit the railway and I noticed recently that most of the bus employees were wearing the black and red uniforms, like the railway workers (seen here opposite top in the 1920s).

Now (in 1931) we can travel by rail or road for 1s 9d (less than 10p) return, in fact we can go to Newcastle in the train and return with the same ticket by bus. As well as the United, there is the County Bus Service, a private concern which runs in opposition to United, and there are many private buses which run to local routes (and private charabancs like the one seen here leaving Woodhorn Road in the 1920s).

Early History of Hirst Welfare and the Booth Cup

Ashington Welfare Football League was launched in 1920 in an atmosphere of excitement for nothing like it had been attempted before. The Junior Division for under-18 year olds began in the October and the Senior Division got under way a month later. By January the following year 45 games had been played.

In the beginning there was great emphasis on underground and departmental teams. Woodhorn Colliery had *two* teams: one from the Low Main Seam and another from the surface workers, called Woodhorn Bank. The timber-yard men at Ashington Pit called themselves Whinny Field, and a team of tankey drivers took the name of Loco United.

Divisional winners in those days played off the finals at Portland Park, home of Ashington FC. In the 1921/22 season, the following played for the Duke Pit, winners of the Senior Division: captain was R. Rand, George Scott, George Jackson, John Collins, Alex Milburn (father of Wor Jackie), Jack Milburn (played later for Leeds United), John Robin, Jack Kirkup (secretary of Ashington Institute, no relation, went on to win a BEM), Ben Tinker (later played hockey for Northumberland), J. Lockyer and J. Tinkler. The runners-up that season had James Leslie Brownrigg in the squad – he later drew cartoons for the Colliery Magazine.

Bothal Pit, winners of the Junior Division, fielded a founder member of the Pitmen Painters in the team, namely Oliver Kilbourn; and Bob Blacklock, who still sings with Ashington Male Voice Choir (2003), was in the same team. The Ashington Welfare select eleven won the Northumberland Junior Cup that same season with this team: Evans, James L. Brownrigg, Tom Sleightholme, C. 'Charlie' Chester, Campbell, Jim Guy, A. Dobbinson, Bill Dawson, R. Crow, George Johnson and Norman Johnstone. The Hirst Welfare was part of Milburn Estates that was sold to Ashington Coal Company (of which William Milburn was a founder member), in 1920 at the knock-down price of £10 per acre. Ten years earlier, the site of Hirst Flower Park and recreation ground, had been sold to Ashington Council for the much more realistic price of £120 per acre.

The Booth Trophy as it was known was presented to the Welfare Sports Club by Mr Freddie Booth (an Ashington Coal Company Agent) at the Club's Annual Gathering in 1932. It had originally been presented by the Ashington Old Pit Co-operative Society to the Recreation Ground Committee in 1887 and had been won three years in succession by the Ashington Football Club who then had the right to keep it, but they presented it to Mr Booth's mother.

In season 1932/33 it was first competed for by the Welfare Club in a knock-out competition and the first winners were Hirst Villa. In season 1933/34 it was won by the Hirst Corinthians and the following season by Hirst 'A'. Hirst

Corinthians then won it two years in succession, but in 1936/37 it was the turn of Hirst Ex-Juniors who brought off the treble by also winning the League and the Challenge Cup. Ashington Electricians (seen here left) performed the same feat in the 1938/39 season. The squad included: R. Youngs (captain), Fred Redpath, Des Mullholland, R. Hancox, Dave Gibson, George Reed, Ossie Sword, J. Strother, J. 'Butcher' Robson, B. Furness, A. Scott and F. Ross.

Ashington Electricians, 1938/39.

Runners-up in 1938/39 were Hirst Ex-Juniors with this team: Tom Angus, A. Brotherton, John Bell, T. Foster, Bill 'Dot' Anderson. Front row: L. Andrews, 'Dancer' Broome, G. Wilkinson, M. Cummings, 'Peasy' Emery and Billy McLean.

Although it was a minority sport, Hirst Welfare had a flourishing Badminton Club. Some of them are seen here at the Trade Union Hall at their 2nd annual dinner dance in 1939. Among those present were: Alf Armstrong, Mrs Harry Armstrong, George Scott, Miss Lily Dockerty, Miss E. Pickering, Harry Smith and Doris Besford. Doubles winners Joe Curry and Miss E. Blandford were joined by R. Patterson and Miss P. Jamieson, plus R. Hindmarsh and Mrs Robson. Music was provided by the Clark Brothers' Band.

Scouting in the 1930s

The 4th Ashington Troop were formed in 1933 and run in connection with the Ashington Parish Church although their headquarters were in the Mission Hall in the Hirst, behind North Seaton

September 1933   THE ASHINGTON COLLIERIES MAGAZINE   Page 253

SCOUT NOTES BY SCOUTER

Road. Their first scouter was a Mr Wilson who supervised the building of their own hut which also accommodated girl guides.

The 'Forst Horst' was one of the strongest groups in the local scouting association, meeting at St George's Hall, Lintonville, often referred to then as the Old Lane. They had a Working Parents meeting every Monday making woolen garments and mats. Leader was Jack Dorgan with assistant Joe Dalkin. The Cub Pack in the 1930s was run by Bob Parks and Tom Pears. A Patrol Leader at the time was Colin McNiven who became the youngest leader of Ashington Council in the 1950s. In 1934, the Rover Scouts built themselves a Den as a copy of a lumberman's cabin with the sides and roof all made of logs with a large open fireplace. Will Melrose of Woodhorn Road was a Rover Scout then. It was he who drew the scouting illustration (above). By 1937, this troop boasted three King scouts, namely G.V. Henderson, V. Scott and J. Cowan, and then there were 190 scouts and cubs attending in the Hirst district.

The Second 'Horst' was connected to the Wesleyan Central Hall at the top of Hawthorn Road. Scoutmaster in the 1930s (and beyond) was George Tomlinson, a deputy at Linton Colliery.

Fourth 'Horst' had the Rev Moxon as a scoutmaster. They met in St John's Parish Hall, Seaton Hirst with Miss B. Tate as leader of the Cubs. In 1933 it was recorded that they were expected to win the Norman Southern Challenge Shield for Handicrafts.

Fifth 'Horst' met at the St Andrew's Mission in Hawthorn Road. George Ferguson, W. Robson and J. Tomlin were in charge in the 1930s. Scouter Ferguson was a keen member of the St John's Ambulance Brigade and this was reflected in the group. A regular visitor was Dr Andrew Irvine who gave displays on First Aid. In February 1933 they held a concert featuring sword dancing from 1st Newbiggin Sea Scouts, while Hector McKinnon, also from Newbiggin, entertained on mouth organ.

A World Scouting Jamboree was held in August 1933. Representatives seen here are William Gibson (District Commissioner), with Jack Dorgan and Joe Dalkin of 1st Hirst.

HIRST GETS DOWN TO BUSINESS

Station Road, Ashington. 7162

Before the First World War there was a distinct split in the town. Ashington and Hirst were two completely separate places, physically bisected by the railway station bridge (which can be seen above around 1920). The men to the west of the railway line invariably worked at Ashington Colliery, and those residing in Hirst, on the east, travelled to Woodhorn or Linton pits. Indeed, the two latter mines merged into one when a new headquarters was found for them on Station Road in the Linton and Woodhorn Miners' Hall. The same name was given to a social club in Woodhorn Road. And at the 'top' end of the town, when Ellington Colliery was opened in 1913, the men living in 'high' Ashington became associated with the new colliery, and a private drinking club – the Ashington and Ellington – was formed, catering for both sets of miners.

Ashington and Hirst were now bursting at the seams as private building overtook that of the Coal Company. Each part was now a self-contained community, catering for the many needs of its inhabitants. In May 1914, the Ashington Urban District Council presented to a House of Lords Committee the following figures showing the number of houses and buildings in Ashington and Hirst:

Houses owned by Ashington Coal Company	3,527
Houses owned by other private owners	2,714
Shops with houses attached	173
Shops	74
Churches	15
Clubs	17
Schools	5
Theatres and Picture Halls	5
Institutes	3
Co-operative Stores	8
Farms	2
Hotels	3
Railway Stations (Ashington and North Seaton)	2
Council Premises, including Hospital	4
Post Office	1
Banks	3
Public Halls	5
Police Station	1
Factory	1
Total	**6,563**

STATION ROAD END. HIRST. ASHINGTON. 1790.

Here we can see how Station Road is filling up with shops around 1920.

Private builders, like two Newcastle brothers, Sid and Richard Oxnard, came to the region around 1900 looking for work, and they found it in plenty. The ACC could not cope with the ever-increasing influx of workers, and it was just the right time for private entrepreneurs to step in. At first the brothers concentrated

on the Hirst, building houses in Castle Terrace and Queen Street. When these were completed they moved to the land next to the railway station, and started on Cresswell Terrace, Council Road and part of Station Road. Sid Oxnard built the end house in

Council offices with Council Road in background around 1915.

Council Road for his wife and family.

His daughter Winnie said later: 'As children we would often play next to the railway station when the miners got aboard the tankey (train) for Linton and Ellington pits. Father would tip the guard and he'd let us travel in a carriage with plush seats – the others had hard wooden benches, and were only used by miners in pit clothes. Mother got up very early each morning to clean the brass nameplate on the outside wall. But with all the fumes coming from the nearby pit heap it was coloured purple in a couple of hours.'

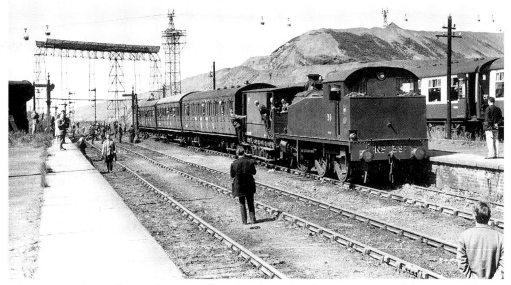

This Ian S. Carr photo shows rail enthusiasts in the 1960s at Ashington with towering pit heaps in the background.

About 1909, Ashington Council decided to merge some of the street names at Hirst and elsewhere in the town. House building until then had been haphazard with streets named after rivers – Mersey, Severn, Medway and Clyde – spreading north from the North Seaton Hotel and Newbiggin Road. These river names gave way to trees such as Sycamore, Chestnut and Maple. Humber Terrace saw its name changed to Hawthorn Road, but the post office still retained its original name. Photo shows Newbiggin Road and it was upwards from here that street names were changed.

When the building of colliery houses at Hirst ceased around 1910 the area took on the shape of a huge grid with 28 houses to each street, separated by eight avenues. Outside privies, coal houses and bin corners bisected streets like Maple and Chestnut, and then a back alley ran the length of the street, often being used as a dumping ground for unwanted furniture. But streets such as Beatrice and Katherine, built a little later than the others, had long enclosed backyards, giving far more privacy. It wasn't until the early 1930s that the Coal Company, after much badgering by the Council, began to install flush toilets. Photo shows an aerial view of Hirst with United bus depot in foreground.

I was born in February 1934 in an upstairs flat at No 63 Hawthorn Road, Hirst, the first child of Jack and Lizzie Kirkup (née Talbot). I am seen here with my parents in the backyard. The spelling of mother's surname is important because half of her siblings of two sisters and eight brothers changed their names to Talbert in later years. Whether it was intentional or by accident is not known.

Being born on a Wednesday, I was destined to become, or so my mother always vowed, 'full of woe'. I do not remember anything of that Hawthorn Road flat, but I do recall the next house we moved to in Monkseaton Terrace, facing out on to Wembley Field. A couple of doors down lived the Maxwells and as a toddler I became friendly with their youngest child then, Heather. An older sister, Peggy, went on to make a name for herself in the field of dancing, both as a performer and then teacher of dance. The Routledge clan also lived in that street.

Old Mick and Young Mick.

I must have been all of three years old when Heather and I locked ourselves in the nettie at the bottom of our backyard. Our tryst was broken by an eye appearing at a knot-hole in the door and my mother's distinctive voice bellowing: 'Whaat are ye two deein' in there?' It was while we were living here in 1940 that my Uncle Manny, who was also living with us, joined the Army. He came home one day in his khaki uniform carrying a rifle which I thought was great. Manny clipped the rifle to his bed while he slept. 'Canna have Jerry comin' over and takin' that, now can we,' he told me.

By the beginning of the Second World War our family had been swelled by another. No it wasn't another child – it was my granddad, old Mick Talbot. He was old Mick and I became young Mick. My mother's father had come to live with us on the death of his wife, Ann (née Cain) at the age of sixty. Having borne twelve children – one died as a baby – her frail body just gave up the ghost the year I was born. The Talbot and Cain clan had come to England from county Mayo at the height of the Irish potato famine in the 1860s. They had lived in County Durham for a time, moving to Tyneside after they were wed in 1884. Old Mick became a miner and, just before the Newcastle-based pit of Montagu where he worked was flooded, he brought his young family to live at 95 Poplar Street, Hirst, where his youngest son, Richard (Dick) was born in 1910.

My father's family lived in Severn Street (later re-named Sycamore) in the early 1900s – he was born in 1902. The Kirkups consisted of parents, Jack and Agnes (née Cassidy), four sons, Larry, Jack, Sidney and Dennis; and four girls, Dorothy, Peggy, Edith and Mary. I am seen here with Uncle Dennis, my mother and Grannie Kirkup at her house at 91 Katherine Street.

When I was five I attended the Hirst South School for a short time, probably because our house in Monkey Terrace was so near. But my mother was a staunch Catholic and it wasn't long before we moved again, this time to an upstairs flat in the second block of even Sycamore, around No 100, as far as I can recall. A canny childless couple, Mr and Mrs Joe Lynch, lived downstairs and the Waughs, including daughter Joyce, lived next door. I was often carried downstairs by my mother during an air raid to sit with the Lynchs under their stairs. Father refused to get out of bed, vowing that the German bombers would never get him and that if he was to die then it would be more comfortable to do so in his own bed.

It was through Joyce Waugh that I was to meet one of the first girls I had a crush on – or perhaps it was the other way around. Joyce's Hirst Park School friend was Nancy Forster who lived in Sycamore Street, even numbers, 3rd block. I was all of seven years old when Nancy and another girl invited me into the Forster toilet at the other side of the backstreet 'to see Mickey Mouse'. As far as I can recollect I didn't see anything remotely resembling a Walt Disney creation. Nancy is on this Park School photo seated far right; Joyce Waugh is behind her, 2nd right.

Churches, Clubs and Council Houses

St Andrew's Parish Church on Hawthorn Road, seen above from the 3rd Avenue side, had humble origins as a wooden building. This was replaced in the late 1920s with the present red-brick church. People probably remember it more from a thirty-year period between the 1940s and the '60s. It was then that St Andrew's had a flourishing choir when Harold Drinkwater and his father were prominent members. But church music wasn't the only kind that reverberated around the holy walls. In the 1940s you were able to listen to Joe Dalkin and his Rhythm Boys at the Sixpenny Hop. As musical fashions changed, so Joe was usurped in the late 1950s by a young rock 'n' roller called Neil Dixon who had the youngsters dancing in the aisles. Hallelujah!

As Hirst was developing, a band of young Methodists, mainly drawn from Ashington, began to hold cottage meetings in the house of James Curtis in Sycamore Street and after that the Store Hall in Hawthorn Road. These services continued until the Hirst School Chapel was built in 1898. A house was rented in Milburn Road in 1902, also for the Methodists. From this grew Thwaites Memorial Chapel on Seventh Avenue (as seen in photo) when adjacent land was bought and plans approved for a schoolroom and chapel. But only the former was built, and the Church grew under the guidance of Pastor W.H. Thwaites.

The Second Avenue Chapel (as seen in photo) was opened in 1900. A Church Hall was built on to it in 1957 and a Porch was added in 1960. These additions cost £5,686 and were paid for from the proceeds of the sale of the Sycamore Street premises to the Salvation Army.

The first Methodist chapel on Woodhorn Road was called the Lesser Hall, built in 1898. Before the First World War, the Reverend Walter Weddell drew the attention of the Methodist Church to the rapidly growing population of Hirst. The mining industry was developing, drawing people from all parts of the country to a town that was to become the 'biggest mining village in the world'.

It was not until after the Great War in 1919 that additions were possible at the Hirst when an old Army hut was bought and erected by the young men – it was to be called the Young People's Institute. With the help of the Newcastle District Coalfields Mission, a Central Hall was planned. The first sod was cut by Mr W. Gray (seen here with young Harry French and Cecil Paton) on 23rd January 1923 and was completed on 21st May 1924.

In 1931, one of the finest organs in the North was brought from the Miners' Theatre in Ashington. Recruited at about the same time was Mr Normanton Barron who became musical director and conductor of various choirs and orchestras associated with the Central Hall which, as you can see, was a magnificent building.

This became the venue for celebrity concerts which filled the Hall. Famous musicians and singers, such as Reginald Dixon and Joan Hammond, brought great pleasure to the humble pit community. The key figure in bringing these artistes to Ashington was undoubtedly Mr Barron.

Council House Building

Much of the green land of Hirst was swallowed up when Ashington Council began to build homes to cope with the influx of mining families into the district. In the 1970s, colliery houses were demolished next to Ashington Pit, and a new estate was built to accommodate those who were moved. What follows is taken from a report by Wansbeck Council Building Department published in 1979.

1923-25	Garden City Villas – 98 houses built
	South Villas – Brinkburn Crescent, Fontburn etc – 142 houses built
1925-27	Park Villas – 58 houses built
1933-38	Bothal Cottages – 85 houses built
1936-38	Aln Street, Coquet, Tweed, Tyne etc – 121 houses built
1945-46	Milton Grove – 24 prefabs built
	Ariel Street – 9 houses built (opposite Hirst Park playing fields)
	Moorhouse Lane – 12 houses built
	Alexandra Road (265-287 plus 112-130) – 22 houses built
1946-48	Woodhorn Villas – 119 houses built
1948-50	North Seaton Road Estate (Bywell, Norham etc) – 300 houses built
1951-52	Alexandra Court – 102 flats built
1952-53	Blyth Terrace – 25 bungalows built
1953-55	Kenilworth Road Estate (Chillingham, Bamburgh etc) – 208 houses built

This Harry Speight photo shows the start of Green Lane house-building in the early 1950s, taken from the railway line.

1955-56	Roseneath Court – 76 houses built
1957-60	More Kenilworth Road Estate (Coupland, Elsdon etc) – 229 houses built
1960-63	Sweethope Estate (Bolam Drive, Linshiels Gardens etc) – 222 houses built

1963-64	Moorhouse Estate – 148 houses built
1965-67	Alexandra Road (part of) plus College Road/College Place, Hesleyside, Kirkley Drive, Simonburn Lane etc – 311 houses
1966-67	Byron Place, Milton Grove etc – 106 houses
1968-69	Following the demolition of some colliery rows (2nd-6th Rows): Cheshire Close, Devon Close, Dorset etc – 317 houses built
1968-75	A massive building programme took place on land opposite the Tech College: Canterbury Close, Norwich, Winchester etc – 430 houses
1969-70	College Road and College Place completed – 24 houses
1975-78	Woodbridge Estate (renamed The Churches) – 270 houses
1975-79	Green Lane Estate (Briardene, Greencroft etc) – 189 houses

Ashington Council had made a disastrous first attempt at providing council houses in the Hirst in the 1920s. Dorman Long concrete houses were bought in at an exorbitant cost of £1,300 each and were erected below Hirst Park. The Council found them difficult to let because of the high rentals. Many had to be let to two families.

After that, council house building continued in a haphazard fashion with the site locations seemingly being dictated more by expediency than forward planning. This resulted in ghettos being formed, especially in the Hirst – a problem that is still with us in 2003.

Opened in 1895, Priestman's Institute (seen here soon after it opened) was one of Hirst's oldest and most integral social centres. Its membership began with 500 men, but by the 1920s this had grown to over 2,000. Some of the early caretakers were Ned Fitzpatrick, Bill Shell, Sammy Morgan and Wilson Graham. Billiards and snooker, as well as darts and dominoes, were provided, including a well-stocked library and a comfortable reading room which took most of the daily newspapers. In the 1960s it was taken over by CISWO, but this fine piece of architecture was deemed unprofitable in the 1970s and, like the Grand Hotel just up the road, it was demolished.

Michael Gray, formerly of Newbiggin Road, was working on the construction of the new Tech College at the bottom of Hawthorn Road in 1958 when he took this photo from a high vantage point on the third storey. This is a view of the first concrete council housing estate (unkindly nicknamed Chinatoon) destined to be demolished shortly after this photo was taken to make way for Sweethope Avenue and other council houses. In the centre are the trees of Hirst Flower Park and in the distance you can spot the smoking chimney of Woodhorn Colliery.

This is a much earlier photo of Woodhorn Colliery taken around 1900 near a crossing that was used next to the Aged Miners' Cottages. The men in knee length 'hoggers' were hewers. The man in centre beside the gate is smoking a clay pipe which he probably took down the pit. Woodhorn was a 'naked flame' colliery until a gas explosion killed 13 men in August 1916.

From the beginning of the 20th century, many Scottish doctors set up practice in the Hirst and Ashington. One such man was Dr McPherson, seen here 2nd left at his retirement from his Lintonville Practice in the 1970s.

STATION ROAD, ASHINGTON

This is the 'Main Street' as many people will remember it in the 1950s. This was a boom time for the town when every shop was taken up along this 100-yard stretch of road. Huge department stores like Arrowsmith's, Shephard's and Doggart's ensured that shopping was done here, within walking distance of residents' homes, and not in anonymous retail arcades.

This was the Hawthorn Road in the early 1930s. Photo above showing all the pot-holes was taken in 1932 before the road was made up, while the one below shows what it looked like when the first concrete was laid the following year. The Central Hall in the distance was a landmark for Hirst folks travelling up this road.

Hirst Clubland

In May 1914, an Ashington Urban District Council survey revealed that, although there were 15 churches in the town, there were no less than 17 workingmen's clubs. That figure later rose to twenty. The majority of clubs at Hirst were opened in a twenty-year period at the beginning of the 20th century. The exact timing and dates are immaterial as many clubs were unofficially open before specific dates were registered. What does seem to be indisputable, however, is that there was great rivalry between the Ashington West End Club and the New Hirst Social Club as to which would be the first in town to open their doors to thirsty pitmen members. Each eventually claimed victory. Photo shows Woodhorn Road in its heyday for clubs in the 1960s.

Five workingmen's clubs stood in what was known as the Low Market area of town, and what we now call Woodhorn Road. First in line next to the Co-op Arcade (although even that building did not exist at the time) was the Hirst East End in premises once used by Moses Sixsmith, a general dealer who later became a prominent club member, winning prizes for his 'show' leeks. Some of

the Hirst residents decided that the club should be open for refreshments the day before the official opening was due to take place; a misdemeanour that was to cost three men a nominal fine when they later appeared in court. In the 1960s it was Dickie Freeman who claimed the leek show prizes; seen here on right with Councillor Larry Lavelle at Hirst Welfare.

Right next door to the East End Club around 1910 was the Hirst Post Office until, with very little alterations to the bare walls and concrete passage, this establishment reincarnated itself as the Northern Club. Two brothers played a prominent part at the East End and Northern clubs. Walter Davison became one of the first stewards at the Northern Club while his brother George Davison took over next door at the Hirst East End. Walter, a one-time pitman at Woodhorn Colliery, had served his apprenticeship behind the bar at the North Seaton Hotel (the White Elephant) when that building opened around 1900. Photo shows bar staff at the Grand Hotel in the 1920s and includes Mr Mitchell who later became steward at the Excelsior Club.

For some reason, Hirst miners allowed a shop to stand between the Northern and their next watering hole on Woodhorn Road: the Linton and Woodhorn. This was so called because the majority of its members were drawn from those two particular pits; Woodhorn being opened in 1894 and Linton a couple of years later. The 'Cree', as it is now known, was originally an offshoot of the Grand Street Club where it got so packed that it was thought an annexe was needed. On a cold day at the L&W the miners could warm their fish and chips on an old-fashioned kitchen range standing behind the central pillar in the main bar.

The Hirst Premier was a grocer's shop originally. A round coke oven stood in the middle of the bar and it was alleged that the furniture had seen better days on steamships and in breakers' yards. Around 1920, the Premier Club extended into the draper's shop next door.

The Hirst Industrial (the Indus) took over from a place called the Shamrock, Thistle and Rose Club (obviously named so as not to offend the Irish, Scots or English). The Indus was rebuilt around 1923, but the long miners' stoppage of 1926 was responsible for a crisis in the club's finances as they were unable to pay the interest charges on a £3,500 loan. It took until 1939 for the members to drink sufficient beer to settle the debt. Opposite page top left: It is seen here in a Reuben Daglish photo taken in the late 1990s.

Way down at the bottom of Woodhorn Road, opposite the original Hirst Castle, was a house built for Dr Goldie in 1894. This was converted into what became better known as the Universal Club or the Varsal. In 1909 it had been called The Royal, probably because of that year's coronation of King George V. After closing in the 1990s and standing unused for a few years, the new millennium saw it revert to a pub, called the 'Hyrste Castle'. Opposite page top right: Shows bar staff and steward at the Varsal in the 1930s when it was simply 158 Woodhorn Road.

This is the team that represented the Hirst Central Club in the Ashington Welfare League in 1952. Back row: trainer Louis Rogers, Bob Middlemiss, Cecil Robinson, Jackie Down, Brian Maitland, Cyril Beddard, Alan Longstaff and Central committee man, possibly Dickie Jarvis. Front row: Jim Hill, Alan White, Michael Kirkup, Jason Young and Jackie Robinson.

Ashington Goes To The Dogs

Many Ashington hands were thrown up in horror in 1936 when the town acquired a Greyhound Stadium at Portland Park, home of the local football team. Up until then, miners of the Hirst had enjoyed a Sunday morning session of whippet racing at the Foxcover or other local fields where bets were struck with opposing owners.

Methodist ministers harangued the pitmen gamblers of the community. None more so than the visiting Rev Percy S. Carden who, on hearing that the United Bus Company had been refused an application to put duplicate buses on to get Hirst folks to the dog track, had this to say: 'What are the things in Ashington I most admire? I admire the wide streets and well-kept gardens. I admire the cleanliness and homeliness of the houses in the colliery rows. I admire the doctors who can be seen at all hours of the day and night assiduously carrying on their ministry of healing. I admire the quiet efficiency of our Ashington undertaker and the reverend way in which neighbours show respect in the hour of death.

The ritual of the tin bath in front of the fire.

'I admire the men I meet coming home from the pits, begrimed though they be, and always think of them as men to whom we owe a debt which we can never pay, for it is one of my fundamental beliefs that a miner should be as well paid and as well housed as a lawyer, a schoolmaster or a parson. I admire the fine work done in our hospital, where doctors, sisters and nurses, scorn delights and live laborious days. And I admire the good work done by our public servants and councillors.

'But I loathe the Greyhound Racing Track, with its hideous totalisator, its crowd of simple greedy fools who prey and are preyed upon by the Gambling Vampire who always gets the blood of the children. I loathe the workingmen's clubs if they be simply drinking clubs, rather than the houses of fellowship and good comradeship they were intended to be by their best-intentioned founders.

This Humphrey Spender image shows a greyhound race in progress at Portland Park in 1938 with totalisator in background.

'But I admire the picture halls and the variety of shows they present – shows which are often well worth seeing though naturally not always so. I admire the Central Hall with its fine imposing front and wonder why the people of Ashington do not appreciate it more; and the churches which in the main are not so well attended as one would desire – and many other things.

'I also admire the decision of the Area Traffic Commissioner to prevent henceforth the duplication of buses on routes used mainly by people who, in more senses than one, are *Going to the Dogs*.'

SOME OF OUR READERS' BABIES.

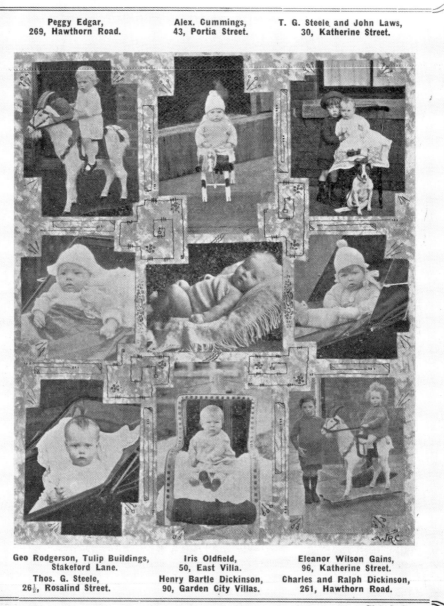

Peggy Edgar,
269, Hawthorn Road.

Alex. Cummings,
43, Portia Street.

T. G. Steele and John Laws,
30, Katherine Street.

Geo Rodgerson, Tulip Buildings,
Stakeford Lane.

Iris Oldfield,
50, East Villa.

Eleanor Wilson Gains,
96, Katherine Street.

Thos. G. Steele,
26½, Rosalind Street.

Henry Bartle Dickinson,
90, Garden City Villas.

Charles and Ralph Dickinson,
261, Hawthorn Road.

Photos by Curry

Some of the toddlers who were featured in the 1926 *Ashington Colliery Magazine*. Those who have survived will be in their late seventies.

SECTION FOUR

DIFFERENT HIRST PERSPECTIVES

ASHINGTON STATION. W.M.

Maurice Hook makes this observation: 'Did the railway line (above) separating old Ashington Town from New Hirst create an 'other side of the tracks' attitude as the town developed over the first half of the 20th century? In housing, the 'top end' had the best private stock where even its colliery houses had huge south-facing gardens, compared with the Hirst's cramped rows. Ashington had the Catholic Church and the earliest consecrated Church of England (The Holy Sepulchre). The Salvation Army had a brick-built Citadel, superior to the Hirst's hut on Milburn Road and the East Villa's Corps on Alexandra Road. The Miners' Theatre had converted to the plushest cinema in town (the Regal) in 1939, although the Hirst had quadruple the number of picture houses. Is it my imagination which suggests that Scout and Girl Guide Troops with the 'Ashington' nomenclature (1st Ashington, 2nd Ashington etc) seemed grander than their Hirst (1st Horst, 2nd Horst etc) equivalents? Most of the bright pupils resident in the top end who passed their eleven-plus went to the long-established Morpeth High Schools, while the Hirsties tended to go to the 'red brick' Bedlington Grammar School. There will (of course) be counter arguments.'

Bill Taylor's Tree
by Diane Green

The tree above stands across the road from The Elephant (at Seaton Hirst). It is a Canadian Poplar, and it is next to the Newcastle bus-stop. You have probably walked past it without giving it a second thought. In 1928, a young man called Bill Taylor and his work mate Charlie Lisle dug a hole in ground as hard as granite with fingers frozen by the north-east wind. They set the tree where it still stands today (1999). Bill is now ninety-three and he still mentally tips his hat whenever he passes that tree. How was he to know that he and the tree would still be around at the end of the century?

A six-foot sapling was brought from Morpeth (probably Matthewson's Gardens) and its resting place was chosen to screen the public lavatories which stood beside the Hippodrome Theatre. Spedding's old post office, the sweet shop, and the dressmakers in the middle, have all been replaced by new buildings. The narrow path to North Seaton is now a wide road into Nursery Park Estate. Bill and the tree have survived the changes.

Bill Taylor's and Charlie's efforts here marked the start of a deliberate policy of tree-building by the Ashington Urban District Council. The back streets (of Hirst) lacked greenery, and the decision-makers on the council wanted to bring into the town some reminders of the surrounding countryside. Trees raised locally from seed were planted along North Seaton Road in the late 1940s (when the new council estate was built there). Bill is justifiably proud of these beautiful trees.

Garden City Villas was planted up and also the road to Newbiggin. People's Park was surrounded by trees. But Flowering Cherries, planted at the bottom of Alexandra Road beside the prefabs, were quickly vandalised; sometimes they were found broken immediately after planting. Yet for some reason there was

less vandalism in the colliery rows (of the Hirst). Photo shows newly-planted saplings on North Seaton Road in early 1950s.

Bill was made foreman-gardener for AUDC soon after he returned from serving in the Second World War. A garden nursery was acquired at the old fever hospital at Pity Me, and trees from there were used to plant up Dr John Noble's garden. The trees planted around Langwell Crescent cricket ground also date from around this time – each one was planted there in memory of a local man who did not return from the war. Later, trees were planted down Hawthorn Road, where residents were given a choice – some decided not to have a tree in their garden. There were those who said the tree-planting scheme would not work, but Bill never lost faith in what he was doing. He knew the community would benefit in the long run.

Bill Taylor (seen right) died soon after the above article was written. The many trees that Bill planted will be his legacy to the Hirst. Diane wrote: 'Of course it was his job to plant them, but for Bill it was more than a job. His heart was always in his work. Bill planted them as a young man looking ahead to the distant future. That his faith was well founded is evident in the trees themselves. Look at them now and say a quiet "Thank You" to Bill and his mates, and to all who were determined to bring trees to the streets of the Hirst.'

'Owwer the Waal is Six 'n' oot'
by Allan Brownrigg

Hirst looking north with Beech Terrace in front and Hawthorn Road on right. Hirst as a suburb was never a concept of great importance in our lives during the 1940s and '50s as it did not seem to have clearly-defined boundaries or a central heart and we did not seem to owe it any allegiance. If anyone asked where we came from the reply was always 'Ashington' and never Hirst. Nevertheless it did exist and the name Hirst was widely spread geographically, as shown by its appearance as an adjective attached to many places and organisations.

Like myself living in Ariel Street, there is no doubt that many of us who lived next to the Hirst Park (and Flower Park), went to the Hirst East Infants, followed by the Hirst South Juniors which was a one class school, although we had four standards and the numbers were very large. In my case 46 or 47 pupils was the norm. Others went to the Hirst North, where they were split into Uppies and Doonies, but I don't know how those decisions were made. I suppose the dividing line between north and south was Third Avenue. PT at the North School, even for girls, was regimental, as seen in this 1940s photo.

The Hirst Park was a wonderful, enormous place, but the authorities made it very difficult to get into. Keeping people out seemed to be their main job. All the time I was young it was surrounded by a tall wooden paling fence with points on the top and with very few gates. Of course palings were often being pulled off, as the youths and miners were never keen on going the long way round. That would give us littlies a chance of getting into the Park and playing cowboys or football and enjoying running around on the grass. There was a proper playground in the Park at the other side but I was discouraged from going there. Danny Scott had died falling off the banana slide, and the other rides were also reckoned to be dangerous with big kids kicking the swings up high and making the Teapot Lid go fast. Also on the other side was Hirst Park Modern School where the big lads and lasses went.

This photo shows a group of us toddlers crawling through a hole in the fence at Hirst Park where we could sneak in. I am on the back left with Melvyn Trevethick; in front is Rychek (Richard) Popek and Colin Furness. It was taken around 1944; you can see where I lived at 168 Ariel Street; the lady in the garden is probably my Aunt Vi (Violet Landels). Rychek was the son of a Polish airman who married Doris (or Doreen) Nesbitt whose parents had a shop on the corner of Alexandra Road. The Furness family lived at number 174 Ariel Street.

Football posts were always the most important part of the Park, moving around from time to time as the goalmouths got too muddy and the grass disappeared. One of the highlights every week was the huge Sunday-morning football games where anyone could play and there were usually about 30 players a side. No elitism there – probably no refereeing either. The game never stopped for long. If there was any dispute, someone would kick the ball and the game would immediately restart while the disputants would have to decide whether to continue arguing or join in the game. It was quite a skill to work out who was on your side. I later learned that people came from far beyond the Hirst to play there.

Our neighbourhood in the early years was defined by the shops as well as the Park. We had Nesbitts, Mills and Hendersons at some time on the corner with Fourth Avenue – if it was Fourth Avenue as, unlike Third Avenue, it was cut off by the Park and I was not aware of its existence until later. Davison's the Butcher was there too for many years. Later my shopping expeditions expanded to include the Store on the corner of Third Avenue, next to the fish and chip shop, Rodway's on Second Avenue for the football paper, Deuchars for bottled

beer, Ron Hedley's for a haircut (sitting on the plank across the arms of the seat) and the Humber Terrace Post Office on Third Avenue for stamps. Where was Humber Terrace? I roamed far but never found it. Early in life, I also got to know the red telephone box at the end of Third Avenue quite well. Nobody I knew had a phone, but sometimes, usually in an emergency, a neighbour needed to ring a relative or a doctor and that seemed to be my job. Why? I don't know but maybe it was because I had somehow mastered the use of Buttons A and B. This photo of Ron Hedley was taken by another barber, Gordon Agan, when Ron was learning the trade in the late 1930s at Gordon's shop on the corner of Hawthorn Road and First Avenue.

Of course at our end of Hirst we were near the country and we often went for walks to Moorhouse Farm, then over the stiles and through the fields, passing the huge crater left by a German bomb, and on to North Seaton Village, which seemed to be well beyond Hirst. At that time North Seaton Hall was still

there, surrounded by trees but decaying and full of squatters. Another path, at the end of Alexandra Road, led on to the Fox Cover and Newbiggin Road and was a favourite site for the illegal pitch and toss school with lookouts posted. This pitch and toss scene is drawn by Vera Hook.

48

Before starting at the South School there was no point in going walking south of Hirst Park as there were allotments and then the South Villas, which had some tough kids and were to be avoided. To the north up Alexandra Road were more allotments beyond East Villas and then the Hirst Welfare, then the miners' cottages before the hill to the Universal. Many walks in that direction took us to Woodhorn, or Newbiggin along the narrow path by the railway line. So Woodhorn Road seemed to be the northern boundary of Hirst, uncertain but yet fixed. On the other hand, post-war Hirst expanded at the eastern and southern boundaries with the building of Alexandra Court and the prefabs respectively. Would there be no end to Hirst? Would it one day reach Newbiggin?

Perhaps because of the fence, or perhaps because Hirst Park was too big, most of our games took place in the street. Football at any time and cricket in season with the local rule 'owwer the waal is six 'n' oot.' Marbles and milk bottle tops were played in the gutter or on any spare land between the houses and hide and seek and knocky nine doors at night under the lamp post. The street did not have much traffic; very few neighbours had a car or motor bike. Regular vehicles down the street were the coal lorries heralded by the coalman knocking on the door. 'Put yer coals in missus?' The bin men also came every week to take away the ashes; also the rag and bone man now and again, giving a few pegs for old clothes. Horses and carts were still around and it was a great treat to cadge a lift from the butcher or the milkman, sitting up high behind the horse.

These carts are loading outside the Seaton Hirst Co-op in Milburn Road around 1910.

One of the annoying things about living east of Hirst Park was the lack of public transport. The centre of gravity seemed to be 'up the street' in Ashington, or at least that is where people gathered, usually to spend money.

The pictures, the shops, the ice-cream parlours, the market, the library, the Harmonic Hall, the Arcade were all up there. It was a long way to Hawthorn Road and even longer to Milburn Road or Woodhorn Road to pick up a United bus to go anywhere. The only comfort for the elderly was the Blue Bus to Linton, which I thought to be the most crowded bus in the country, but at one time it was a lifeline for getting up to Woolworths or the Regal and, later in life, further on to Linton. Always it was full to overflowing, but even worse coming back. The familiar cry was, 'Shove up Hinney and let a few more on.' I don't know how the conductor managed to collect the fares and I don't know why they didn't put another bus on. Maybe there was a cause and effect there. Jack Nesbitt drove the Linton bus for many years, seen here at High Market where he parked the bus on waste ground.

Hirst Park, Ashington.

The move to Hirst South County Primary School opened up new regions of Hirst to explore. First of all, twice every day the Flower Park, south of Hirst Park, had to be negotiated and the Parkie avoided. Even more restrictions there, such as not walking on the grass and keeping out of the shrubs, meant we had to be alert at all times as it was hard to keep to the paths day after day. Then onto Hawthorn Road and there were many choices from that point. At the bottom we had the bare windswept Wembley Field where the Hirst South boys used to practise their football skills in the games period and prepare to beat arch rivals Hirst North A and Hirst North B. The southern boundary of Hirst was never too clear. It was obvious where North Seaton was (down the Dene past the Hipp and over the line and turn left) but Seaton Hirst was another matter. It seemed to be the area around St John's Church, so that was probably Hirst too.

There were more restrictions at Hirst South such as keeping off the coke heaps and not going beyond the gates of the Girls' School. Also there were new teachers to contend with. We exchanged Miss Fish for Miss Clarkson, who seemed to detest anyone going to the pictures on Sundays. She would ask the boys who had done such a terrible thing and those who owned up would be beaten on the legs with a ruler. Why were these boys so truthful? It happened every week. Perhaps the consequences of lying were worse, but I can't

St John's Church is seen just beyond the grave of sailor Samson Main who died of wounds inflicted aboard HMS *Wessex* in the Great War.

remember what they were. Next was Mr Patterson, whom we were sorry to see leave to go to Ayrshire. He probably taught me many things but for some reason, how to be a cricket scorer stands out. I think he was followed by the well-known Jack Mather, a councillor. Then in the higher standards we had Mr Andy Foreman, who had the patience and drive to turn us yelling boys into an award-winning choir that sang on the radio once. Good records were kept and he motivated us to do well in tests by comparing us with previous years. Yes, there was a sense of achievement in beating the class of '47.

My view of Hirst changed again on my admittance to Bedlington Grammar School after the eleven-plus exam. My focus for most of the day changed to south of the Wansbeck, but I walked over much of Hirst to get my buses there and back. A bike with gears also helped to widen horizons and soon almost all of Northumberland was within reach. Yet I found something I had not known before. The fame of The Welfare had spread far beyond Hirst and many came from nearby places like Stakeford and Cambois to use its facilities. The gym was in demand on any night and on any Saturday there would be perhaps half a dozen football games going on, all at the same time. What a feast! Of course my favourite was Hirst Park Rangers.

The Welfare was also the centre of sports attention for boxing and many well-supported track and cycling events. Once a year, children would march from all over Ashington to attend Children's Sports Day, when we would be given a shilling, some fruit and a balloon. Once Hirst Welfare was the centre of attention for the whole country when the National School Games were held there in 1954. That must have been a great coup for the Hirst: many of the locals shared beds or got shifted out to relations in order to put up athletes from all over the country. My family had a shot putter from Surrey who must have found it all very strange and I often wonder what became of him.

What became of me is another story.

A Strange Kind of Pride in the Hirst
by Ray Wear

Though I was born and bred in the Hirst, I was never quite sure whether it began at the Grand Corner or the Central Hall. I knew where it ended though, because I lived in Woodhorn Road and there was nothing beyond that, only the allotments and Woodhorn Pit.

This is a Woodhorn Road scene, drawn by Julian Trevelyan in 1937. Bit of artistic licence here, I fear, with drunken miner depicted lying in gutter.

Born in 1927, my first impression of life was of a proggy mat by the fireside. It was lovely to sit on, to roll about on, or fall down on when my little legs gave out, far better than the lino that covered the rest of the kitchen floor. Proggy mats seem to have occupied a large part of my life till I finished school and got a job. My Dad got a lungful of gas during the 1914-18 War and was seldom able to earn a fair living wage, so my Mother took up mat-making in an attempt to keep us alive. We must have been amongst the most hard-up families in the Hirst.

Being a dedicated mat-maker, Mother was a regular customer at Paddy's Market (down Lintonville) looking for cast-offs to cut up for clippings. She would often discover something at the market that would just about fit me for school; sometimes it just about did, and if it didn't she could always alter it or turn it into a mat.

It occurred to me in later years that whatever I had learned at school had been gathered in somebody else's cast-offs. But then it didn't matter much – all the bairns in our back lane looked scruffy; some had to stay off school when it rained. There was no shame in that, only sorrow.

Leaving school was a great event in my life. I got a job for twelve-and-sixpence a week (62^1/$_2$p). That was a big boost to our family finances. My Mother could pay the bill at the Store on time and I could watch a Gene Autrey film at the Piv and buy a bar of Cadbury's Marzipan at Ernie Houston's shop for tuppence. I was rich.

Central Hall, Ashington.

Though my Dad ended his working days on the screens at Ashington Colliery, he had a strange kind of pride in the Hirst. 'They just have numbers on the streets at the top end,' he would say. 'We've all got names down here.' But we had far more than that. We had the Central Hall (above) and the Flower Park: a little patch of beauty in a wilderness of dust. We had the Lonnen and the Larky Field, and the Narrow Path where Shanks' Pony would carry us down to Newbiggin sands to blow all the cobwebs away. Whey, man, it was better than Blackpool.

But the proggy mats are museum pieces now, like the hard-working women who progged them; like the banners that waved on Picnic days and the folk who cheered them all; like the bands that marched with pride in their hearts because pride was all we had. It is nice to sit in the Park in the sun now and remember the Hirst as it used to be – that proggy-mat world, the bread tins on the fender, and the bairn that marvelled at the chimney wind before it all blew away.

Mother called our house, 'Greystones'
by Malcolm Mackenzie

I was born at No 27 Park Villas when my father managed the Ashington & Ellington club. We then moved into the West End club in the High Market. It had its own house on the premises which, to me in those young days, was huge. My mother decided to buy a house in Welbeck Terrace, number 3, next to a shop. This was in 1939, just before the outbreak of war. When we moved in, we had a visit from the builder, Mr Cooper who told us that, although he had no formal education, he had built most of the stone houses in the vicinity. The building blocks were made by his own people from a mould, and the houses became known as Cooper's Castles because of the way the blocks were laid, one vertical, one horizontal. For some reason, mother called our house 'Greystones'. I had that surname for years.

This is a photo of me in our garden in Welbeck.

At the end of Welbeck on Milburn Road, there was a Spiritualist Chapel where séances were conducted on a weekly basis. Next to us at number 4 lived Mrs Carr, a well-known fortune teller. So we were caught between the spirit world as it were. One of Mrs Carr's sons was Wilf, of Carr's the Jeweller fame. If you can imagine where Welbeck is, between it and Garden City, there is, or was, a narrow path. This linked Milburn Road with the Old Road, or should I say, the Comrades Club. At weekends that path was our form of entertainment at home. Saturday and Sunday lunch-times were the busiest. Mother had nicknames for most of the passers-by. We had four bay windows at the front, so nothing was missed. Most of the names are unrepeatable, (you had to know the woman to appreciate this) but I'll give you a couple: 'The egg-me-on man.' He sold eggs around the houses. 'He stoops to conquer.' Speaks for itself. 'Dot and carry one.' Had a limp. I'll leave it at that.

During the second war, looking from the back yard at number 3, you could see the air-raids on the docks at Blyth. The end house of Rowlington Terrace had a long garden, and people used to line up at the wall watching the searchlights, tracers, flares, and anti-aircraft batteries in the Blyth district. One night a plane dropped a bomb on Soppitts scrapyard down the Old Road. We heard it overhead and then the scream as the bomb dropped, then silence. Mother rushed out into the street shouting 'Oh, my God, there's a bomb in the garden.' She then got her eye on a man on our coalhouse roof. She asked him what he was doing, and he just said that he couldn't remember getting up there.

It's hard to describe the people in Welbeck, they came from all walks of life. Some of the names I remember included: the Robinsons – Mrs Robinson paid us a visit most nights and gave us a laugh. She used to say a lot of her words wrong, like Errol Flynn and his 'yagget'. That well-known singer, 'Marsy Lansy'. And going on holiday to 'Chetlenham'. There were the Wallaces, Mains and Turnbulls – Mrs Turnbull was deaf and her brother was deaf and dumb; and the Langans, just to name a few. The last dozen or so houses at the other end were flats. In one of those, you could go up the back stairs, arrive on the landing, and continue down and out the front door. Different.

What I liked about Welbeck was how handy it was to the shops on Milburn Road. We played a lot at Pity Me (near the Isolation Hospital, seen below) which was just a short walk. I was in the fish shop one night in Milburn Road, and the ginger tom-cat belonging to the owner was walking along the front of the fryer. The next minute there was a puff of steam and without a sound it went to one of its other lives. I've never seen a shop cleared as quickly as that night. One night, during the war, two of us got together and put some carbide in a Federation beer bottle with some water, and screwed the cork on it. We placed it against a wall in the street. After five minutes, nothing, so we decided to investigate. Me being the brave one, I was behind the leader. Just as he bent down to pick it up, Bang! We were both hit by flying glass, he got most of it. Thinking a bomb had dropped, the poor folks in Welbeck and Titchfield raced into their shelters. We weren't exactly local heroes after that night.

All in all, Welbeck Terrace was a great place to grow up, plenty of kids to play with, even if mother used to call the house 'Tiny Tots Stores'. The living room was small, but we had a big front room which, like a lot of people, we seldom used. In spite of it being the war years, and my brothers and sisters being away from home, I remember a lot of good times.

Isolation Hospital nurses. Back row: Woods, Willis, Hunt. Front row: Williams and Best.

55

Leave the Black Sergeant to me
by Norman Hadland

Norman Hadland arrived on the streets of Hirst Ashington in the 1950s riding a second-hand bike purchased from Bobby Gray's salerooms. A Cheshire lad by birth, previously, he had served nine years as a Royal Marine. This is what he made of the Pit Town:

A Bob Each Way.

Although a native of north Cheshire ... and despite its (Hirst) history of strikes and hard times, I found that the people were as friendly towards the 'Polis' as they were to everyone else. Although one afternoon I was cycling along First Avenue when a complete stranger shouted to me: 'Just Asleep and Half Awake.' I thought he was referring to my mental state until I discovered later that I had been given the names of two horses running that day – they both won!

As there were few lollipop men employed at the time, we were required to assist children crossing the road to school. Far more children went home at dinnertime then than nowadays, so this was a four-times-a-day job.

Periodically, a pile of dog licence enquiries were received at the Police Station. Enquiries had to be made at all houses where dog licences had been taken out and not renewed. This was done between duties and often took several weeks to complete. In the majority of cases it was found that the dog had died, but where a dog was over six months and was kept in the house without a current licence being in force then a summons was issued.

All summonses had to be served personally by a policeman. Warrants were issued by the beat constables. I executed my first warrant in Chinatoon (unsavoury part of Hirst) where the offender was more used to the procedure than I was. When I knocked on the door he said: 'Hev ye got ya bike, son?' He then mounted his own cycle and we rode side by side to the Police Station. But he was soon released on bail and pedalling homewards. Once I was embarrassed when arresting a householder with whom I had become friendly for non-payment of rates. He produced the required cash, saying: 'Divvent worry, maraa. It's me system. Aa nivvor pay until they issue a warrant, so Aa keep me money in the bank, gerrin' interest, like.'

The majority of recorded crime in Hirst was the theft of pedal bicycles, most of which were found abandoned and returned to the owner. It was often difficult to obtain a description of a stolen cycle: 'Whey, it's a pit bike – surely ye knaa what a pit bike looks like!' Further conversation would reveal a distinguishing feature such as a broken pedal or no back mudguard. This is me with a pit bike at Woodhorn Colliery Museum in 1998.

Three detectives from the Ashington Police Station were responsible for handling the more serious crimes. Perhaps the best known was Ned Givens who had a remarkable knowledge of the local population and the habits of criminals. Two cars, without radio equipment, were based at Ashington, one being a Morris Eight. These vehicles were only used for a definite purpose which could not be performed on foot. Whilst on attachment to CID, I walked many miles with Detective Givens, including an enquiry at North Seaton Colliery which did not justify the use of a motor vehicle.

On Thursday mornings, one PC at Ashington was detailed to meet a wireless-equipped police car and a posse of NCB security officers outside the Trustee Savings Bank in Station Road where a large amount of cash was collected and delivered as wages to local collieries. At holiday times, the arrival at the back door of the bank on a Wednesday morning had to be supervised as the miners' holiday pay cash arrived in two Navy-type kitbags. Securicor, Group 4 and the like had not begun to invest in crime.

Routine patrols made use of 'conference points' where officers were required to attend once an hour and remain for at least five minutes. These 'points' were made up of eight police telephone pillars situated throughout the town: there were two Dr Who-type Tardis boxes, in Woodhorn Road and in Newbiggin Road near the White Elephant; and two small police offices in Seventh Avenue and Woodhorn Villas; and at public telephone boxes; and one at Ashington Colliery telephone exchange.

On Saturday nights the late-shift constables had to remain on duty for an extra half hour so that there was a police presence until things quietened down after the pubs

and clubs closed down at 10 pm. Sometimes we were warned by telephone of likely trouble on the last train from Blyth. We would stand at Ashington Railway Station to meet revellers from the Roxy dancehall, although there was rarely trouble by today's standards.

Probationary constables were assigned to a particular sergeant and I was fortunate to be under the wing of Sgt Charlie Wilson, known locally as 'The Black Sergeant'. A popular saying amongst the 'tough guys' of the town was: 'Aye, 'nd leave the Black Sergeant to me.'

Charlie Wilson is seen 4th left accepting a cheque on behalf of the Boys Club from Mrs Alec Cummings at the Harmonic Hall in the 1950s. Others on photo include: Mr and Mrs George Storey, Mrs Wilson, Alec and Mrs Cummings, David Absolom, Police Inspector and Mrs Mackintosh and Mr and Mrs Bart Poxton. In rear is piano player Dick Slaughter.

The Harmonic Hall itself was built in the 1890s and soon became home to some of the area's best musicians. Ashington and Hirst boasted many brass bands, some representing various pits, such as the Duke Pit Band, while others were attached to organisations, such as the Hirst Salvation Army Band. The Harmonic was leased in the 1940s by an Italian named Marchi who installed a number of billiard tables. The lease was taken over in the late 1950s by Alec Cummings (seen in photo above) who restored the Hall again as a place of music and dance. It later became the town's first nightclub – The Three Ones – managed by Ronnie Harrison.

SCHOOLDAYS AT THE HIRST

John Paterson was born in Eyemouth, Berwickshire, and orphaned at the age of one when his father and elder brother were lost in the 1881 Great Disaster in that fishing village when scores of men were drowned while fishing in the North Sea. John became a teacher and came to the Hirst area where he met and married Ellen Cook of North Seaton in 1905. He is seen with his Class 6 boys at Hirst North School from around that date. The large white collars worn by some boys were not for decoration – they were to highlight any lice that dropped from their heads. Gassed during active service in the First World War John died at an early age in 1928.

Hirst North School

What follows are some eyewitness accounts of the early days of Hirst North School.

'I officially opened the log book for Hirst North School today, 18th May 1896. A week later, two school managers, Mr Edmond Southern and Mr Henry Richardson, officials of the Ashington Coal Company, came to inspect the qualifications of the staff: Mr H. Carr, Mr William Green and the Misses Elizabeth Smith, Jane Sample, Elizabeth Green and J. Crawford.'

Signed H. Clough (first Head at Hirst North)

'I have examined Standard One in Number and Reading and I find many have no idea of either. The majority of the class is in a very backward condition. There are two classes without teachers and attendance is bad with 305 present out of a total of 380. On 26th March (1909) I closed the school for three weeks on account of an epidemic of measles. A sad occurrence resulting in the death of two scholars happened during the Easter holidays. Maria Harris was fatally burnt and Jane Ann Jordan died from the effects of measles.'

Joyce Williams (Head of Girls 1909)

'Where we lived (Woodhorn Colliery) was a long way off any schools in Ashington, but when it became time for me to begin school (1911) I went to Hirst North. Together with my sister Rhoda, Hilda Mawson and Cissie Easton, we had a long walk, turning into Hawthorn Road, and along Second Avenue into the school. One day the road from the Hirst Castle was absolutely flooded, and after we came home for dinner – which we did every day – we couldn't get back for the afternoon session. We wore little pinafore dresses, and if they got wet there was nowhere in the school to dry clothes, although they did have hot-water pipes.'

Vida Sample

Vida Sample seen in the 1950s coaching girls in verse speaking.

'In June (1913) several cases of Scarlet Fever occurred. Attendance was poor due to this and also to negligence on the part of parents. We re-opened the school after summer vacation on 18th August but attendance was very poor; the general excuse being "not returned from holidays". As the lavatories are being rebuilt and consequently very inconvenient, the school will close at 11.35 am and 3.40 pm on each day until Thursday. We transferred our first girls (130) to Hirst East School on 1st September (1913).'

Joyce Williams
(Note: the Hirst East School opened its doors for the first time in 1913)

'In February (1919) school re-opened after six weeks on account of epidemic and Christmas Holidays. Attendance only fair, and on 6th May, just because of a downpour of rain, it was disgraceful. Many of the absentees live almost at the school door. Present 281 out of 362. Children are staying up far too late at night, and are too sleepy to learn. Every week there are many absences because girls oversleep themselves. I blame the parents.'

Joyce Williams

'When I was a pupil at the North my father worked at the pit as a six-and-ninepence-ha'penny shift man. And there were six of us lads to bring up on that wage. In 1923 there was quite a commotion when a lad called Swinhoe walked on his hands from the bottom end of the school yard right up to the school building – it must have been all of 100 yards. In those days we sat in class on long wooden planks with room for eight boys, and we used a sloping bench to write upon.'

Bob Wedderburn (musician and teacher at Hirst North)

Bob Wedderburn is seen here 2nd right on his transfer from Hirst North as acting Headmaster to Stannington First School as Headmaster. From left: Miss Taylor, Mrs Enid Wedderburn, young Brian Robinson and Roy Henderson and far right is the new Head of Hirst North Boys, Mr Nat Graham.

'I was chosen to hold a massive banner, a kind of red swathe, together with another girl, because we were the tallest. All the children marched under the banner, singing *London Bridge is Falling Down*. This was in the Miners' Theatre in 1924. It must have been Empire Day.'

Gladys Davies (née Boutland)

'Every night I still say the prayer I learned at the North School: "God bless the house from thatch to floor/and twelve Apostles guard my door/And four good Angels guard my bed/Two at the foot and two at the head."'

Lily Freebody (née Wilson)

'I didn't go to school until I was seven years old. My mother kept me at home until the School Board man called. My teacher was Miss Laverick.'

Harry Gledhill

'My mother took me down to the North School when I was about six (1930). She had knitted me this woollen outfit, top and shorts, and I remember crying my eyes out – because I was different from the other lads, you see.'

Jackie Milburn

Scotsman William Patterson took his first teaching post at Hirst North Boys School. Here are some of his notes as transcribed by his daughter S.A. Barnes:

I was assigned to commence work at the end of August 1930, and was given an unstreamed class of sixty 9-year-old boys. The two senior classes were taught in an old Army hut situated in the school yard. In those rooms there was barely room for a teacher's desk as children's desks filled the room. Plans of work and notes of lessons had to be handed to the headmaster each Monday morning. The teaching was formal, and the three Rs were most important, though facts had to be learned in all subjects including history, geography and nature study.

The children's work had to be marked daily – a lot was expected of you – and the Head delighted in looking through the pupils' work and spotting errors that the teacher had failed to correct, thereby having the opportunity to point them out to his assistant in a most superior manner. (Note, one of the head teachers then was Albert Chambers who is listed on the 1901 census as living at number 8 Hawthorn Terrace with his wife Mary Ann, daughter Edith and son Albert.) He had been used to teaching children up to the age of 14 years, but with reorganisation he was left as Head of the junior school. The new purpose-built secondary school for 11 to 14-year-olds (Hirst Park) was referred to by him as 'Ashington University'. It seemed impossible to get close to him, so when he retired there were no regrets.

The newly-appointed man (Mr Hamilton took up his post in Christmas 1932) was a younger man in his early forties, firm, hard working, and sympathetic to children and teachers. To me he was a very helpful person. From my point of view, the place became more like a school than a factory, although teaching there was still very hard work. Many of the children came from poor homes and some came to school barefoot throughout the year. Some came from shack-like dwellings with few amenities, although some were very well cared for – others experienced real poverty. The effects of low wages and of the Miners' Stoppage of 1926 were there for all to see.

Luckily, I found friendly and comfortable lodgings in Hirst Ashington with people who had moved from Fletchertown. Within a few days I had joined the

Ashington Rugby Club and played for over three years, helping them to win the Northumberland Senior Trophy in season 1932/33. There was a friendly social atmosphere at the club and facilities (at the Rec) for training and changing were excellent.

This is some of my class from 1935.

Any feelings of aggression or frustration (at school) could be dissipated in the game itself. Swimming at newly-opened Baths (1931) and tennis in the local (Hirst) Park provided pleasurable escape from the demands of marking books during the evenings of term time.

Here are details of six of the male teachers at some of the Hirst Schools who will be remembered by boys who attended school in the 1940s and '50s.

JACK CAIRNS After serving in the Navy in the Great War, Mr Cairns began teaching at Hirst East School where he remained for the rest of his teaching career. He lived in a colliery-scheme house near the railway line purchased with the help of National Association of Schoolmasters of which he was a founder member in Hirst. As an honorary Lt Commander RNVR, Mr Cairns gave a lifetime of service to the community and to Ashington Sea Cadets in particular.

ANDY FOREMAN Born in 1903 at Greenhaugh but spent his youth living in the Rose and Thistle, Alwinton (it is believed the pub is still in the same family). His teaching career began at Hirst South School in 1923 and he remained there until 1953. During his lifetime, Andy participated in Sport, Gardening and Art – he was one of the founder members of the Ashington Group of Painters and some of his work is displayed at Woodhorn Colliery Museum and in a book called *Pitmen Painters*. However, it was his love of Music that was instrumental in Andy leading his boys' choir to win many competitions. He was also a member of the Newcastle Morris Men, and trained many of his pupils in the art of Morris Dancing.

JOHN McHUGH John attended Morpeth Grammar School and then served in the 1914-18 War in the Durham Light Infantry serving in France where he was wounded. He went to Bede College and then into teaching at Hirst East School where he remained until 1928. That year he moved across to Hirst Park under Charles Hemmingway, it was there Mr McHugh became deputy head, holding this post until he retired in 1964. Jack created a record that might not be beaten – he never missed a single day at school in his entire career either as a pupil or a teacher.

JACK TUCKER The son of a Cornishman, he began as a pupil teacher at the old Bothal School then taught at Hirst East from 1923-28, moving from there to Hirst South until 1942. He then moved to Hexham but returned to the Hirst to take the headship at the South School where he remained until retiring in 1962.

ALEXANDER ROBSON CUTTER Began his teaching career at Hirst North in 1908 becoming acting Headmaster there in 1921. He spent the next seven years as First Assistant Master at Hirst South before going to Hauxley as Headmaster, retiring in 1950 at the age of sixty.

Four founder members of the Ashington branch of the National Association of Schoolmasters were presented with silver tankards in October 1976. From left: Mr J.W. Robertson, Mr Jack Tucker, Mr L. Cooper (national president), Mr John McHugh and Mr Jack Cairns.

JAMES E. WOOD After leaving Morpeth Grammar School, Jim became a pupil teacher at Barrington then served with the armed forces in Palestine during the 1914-18 War. He then began teaching at Hirst South School with Alex Cutter, George Wood, W. Nichol, George Coxon and Andy Foreman. In 1926 he went to

Three faithful childhood companions, Mary Laing, Audrey Stimpson and Audrey Nesbitt, were present at the Hirst North Centenary in 1996, displaying my *Uppies & Doonies* book.

Hirst East where he joined Jack Tucker, Jack Cairns, W. Armstrong and J. Archbold. In 1943 he became Head at Netherton Colliery School and completed his service between 1945-57 as Head of Newbiggin Secondary Modern where he was succeeded by Billy Bell in 1957. Jim Wood died in 1966.

'In September 1933, three friends, Mary Laing, Audrey Nesbitt and myself (Audrey Stimpson) were fast-tracked from Hirst East Infants School to Hirst North Junior Girls School before we were seven years old, and we began a five-year stint at the Junior School. At that time the Hirst North building was divided into four schools: a boys and girls school on the ground floor, and the same on the first floor. A separate building housed the Mixed Infants. Mr Hamilton and Mr Hickling were Heads of the boys, and Miss Sproat and Miss Smith were Heads of the girls. The inevitable question on hearing that you attended the 'North' was: "Are ye an Uppie or a Doonie?" The 'uppies' feeling very superior by reason of their being 'above' the others, no doubt. The intake depended on the catchment area. Those living west of Hawthorn Road to the railway line, bounded by Third Avenue, became 'doonies', and those east of Hawthorn Road, with the same southern boundary, became 'uppies' with the excellent Miss Smith as Headmistress. There were six classes in the school then: Miss Kate Anderson took Std I, Miss Bruce Std II, Miss Vida Sample Std III, Miss Purdy Std IV2, and Sally Kennedy took the slow learners. Another important member of the school was Mr Rutter the caretaker, a rather frightening figure who seemed to spend all his time shovelling coal into the cellar for the central heating boilers.'

Audrey Stimpson (who returned to teach at the same school)

The teaching staff of Hirst North Girls School. Back row: Audrey Stimpson, Margaret Richardson, Connie Dent, Connie Hall. Front row: Sally Watling, Ethel Kirsop, Vida Sample, Isobel Smith (Head), Cissie Greenan, Grace Clark and Dorothy Bell.

'I went to the North School and played for the junior football team. We didn't have strips and just played in anything we, or our mothers, wanted to. Just after the Second War, the school bought some red shirts, and one of the lady teachers made a set of black shorts from the blackout curtains.'

*Sir Bobby Charlton
(Seen here later when
capped for England
Schoolboys in 1951)*

'Bobby's flair for football became really obvious when he was about nine years old, and no one was happier than me to see it developing. Football had been an escape route from pitwork for so many of my family, and I wanted Bobby to at least have the same chance. So when at the age of ten he was picked to play for Hirst North Juniors, it was hardly a surprise, but I was still delighted for him, and even more so when he was made captain.'

Cissie Charlton

'We had occasional examinations by the school doctor and dentist. By far the most regular to visit was the School Nurse before whom we lined up and had our heads examined for lice or 'dickies' as we called them. Those who were infested were excluded until the offending lice were removed. Most homes had a special narrow-toothed comb for removal of the eggs of the lice, and also some very strong *Derbac* soap.'

Audrey Stimpson

School's Log 4th September 1939 – 'As a state of War exists as from yesterday, Sunday, the school is closed to scholars for one week. Teachers will still come in; work is proceeding sandbagging the building, particularly Mr Hickling's office and department which is the Warden's Post and ARP Centre ... instructions received to keep the school closed until air-raid shelters have been provided ... attempts are being made by staff to find private accommodation where children can carry on with their schoolwork.
17th October 1939 – 'Air Raid Warning at 1.55 pm; children immediately dispatched to their homes. Two Nazi reconnaissance planes shot down over north-east coast. All Clear sounded at 2.35 pm.'

'I attended the Hirst North School between the ages of seven and eleven from 1938 to 1942. During the bad winter of 1941, if your group was the last to be released at playtime you never got out of the cloakroom because of a constant hail of snowballs. On occasion, each group (uppie or doonie) elected a 'champion' for a big fight after school which took place between the fronts of Sycamore Street (next to Donnison's shop). It must have been disruptive, even frightening, for the residents to have hundreds of yelling schoolboys cheering on the two combatants ... who simply wrestled.'

Maurice Hook

School Log 5th September 1945: 'Robert Brown accidentally fractured his left leg below the knee. Miss Lowes brought him in from the yard. Mr Stoker English applied a splint, and Miss Allison cycled to Ashington Hospital (no phones in those days) to request an ambulance which arrived promptly. As both parents were away from home, a message was left next door.'

Extract from *News Post*, 19th May 1947: 'Under their tutor Miss Vida Sample, a team of four girls from Hirst North entered and won the team reading competition which took place in the Central Methodist Hall, Newcastle. The team was Jean Erskine, Shirley Williams, Patricia Barrass and Lorna Mavin. Another team of Hirst girls won first prize, too: Patricia Keegan, Dorothy Wilkinson, Shirley Richardson and Patricia Regan.'

Here we have another 1950 winning team from Hirst North: Muriel Hall, Ray Harbottle, Sheila Gray and Jackie Harrison.

School Log 1st April 1949: 'Following an interview with the Area Panel, Robert Charlton, born 11/10/37, will attend Bedlington Secondary School after the summer holidays. (Note: Sir Bobby, after passing the eleven-plus examination, should have gone to Morpeth Grammar, but they only played rugby there.)

Ashington Advertiser 28th May 1949: 'A lot has been said of the senior side of schools' football, but not much has come to notice of the junior side. Hirst North Junior team is, however, making sports' talk. They ended the present season in this fashion: Played 14, Won 14, Lost 0, Goals for 60; Goals against 4. During the present season four boys have been selected for East Northumberland games: Harry Dodd, Robert Charlton, Alan Lavelle and Derek Edgar. Information is that Charlton, a nephew of the brothers George, Jack, Jim and

Stan Milburn, is one of the finest and cleverest footballers of his age ever seen in this area. Dodd is a nephew of Ashington FC left-back, John 'Pop' Dodd.'

The under-11 East Northumberland team at their home ground of Bedlington Station Welfare. Back row: Colin Stephenson, Bob Whitehead, Ken Millican, Bill McCafferty, ? Harrison, Bill Dodds. Front row: Andy Johnson of Lynemouth, 'Mut' Taylor of Barrington, Tom Harrison, Bobby Charlton and David Wrightson. Last three from Hirst North School.

In October 1950, Hirst North School underwent another change of structure. With the opening of the Hirst East (1913) and Hirst Park (1928) the North's school roll began to fall. It was decided to amalgamate both girls' departments, also boys A and B joined under the Headship of Mr Redvers Truman.

Adapted from School Log: 'After interviews in June 1957, Miss Florence Buck from Choppington School beat off the challenges of Miss Ivy Whitelaw (then at Blyth Infants) and Mrs Green of Stakeford School, to become Head of Junior Girls at Hirst North. A few months later Miss Buck learned that she was to lose one member of staff as the school roll had dropped to 375. Miss Mollie Taylor volunteered to become redundant.' Photo shows Florence Buck (left) and her sister Lena who lived in Wansbeck Road.

Right: These girls attended Hirst North in 1937. Back row: Gertie Carlton, Susan Dodds, Joyce Mather, Isobel Middlemiss, Joyce Croft, Alice Parry. Front row: Gladys Birchall, June Cowell, Rhoda Russell, Betty Bruce and Mary Partis.

Below: Hirst North Dinner Ladies, 1943. School dinners began about this time, being cooked for all schools at central kitchen in Pegswood. These ladies worked in the Hirst North Infants both during and after the Second World War. Back row: Mrs McFarlane, Mrs Erskine, Mrs Simpson, Mrs Maggie Brown. Front row: unknown, unknown, Katherine Margaret Pearson and Mrs Rhoda Cassidy.

Hirst North Girls win Dickens Banner, 1948. Lorna Black (née Mavin) recalls: 'I remember the Verse Speaking competitions at the Lit & Phil in Newcastle. My own moment of glory came in 1948 with four other Hirst North Girls.' From left: Lorna Mavin, Stella Moyes, Jean Erskine, Pat Barrass and Shirley Williams.

Hirst North Girls, 1950. Back row: Sheila Johnson, Eva Horn, Debbie Rogers, Gladys Purvis, Gillian Hogg, Alice Purdy, Rita Adamson, Brenda Routledge, Norma Main, Ann Laws, Doris Henderson. Middle row; unknown, Nancy Dixon, Shirley Anderson, Pat Waldock, Mary Herron, Eleanor Clements, Alice Gordon, Sybil Cardno, Dylis Arkle, unknown, Jean Stephenson, Joan Pearson. Front row: Brenda Dixon, Marlene Gray, Ann Stephenson, Lillian Clinton, Florence Stewart, Miss Clark, Rosalind Tait, Ann Roberts, Margaret White, Ruth Hare and Pat Hostler.

Hirst North Infants, 1952. This group were on their way to the annual
Children's Gala, held that year at Hirst Welfare. They are seen at the corner of
2nd Avenue and Alexandra Road being guided by two NUM men, Dick
Sanderson and Tommy Davison.

Hirst North Girls, 1952. Back row: June Pawlyn, Ruth Eastlake, Elsie Harper,
the Morton Twins, Joyce ?, Elsie Stafford, Rene Littledale. Middle row includes:
Lydia Storey, Mary Hudson, Jean Adams, Jean Pearson, Diana Hogg, Gladys
Hall, Ann Davison, Ina Laws. Front row: Jean Milburn, unknown, Joyce ?, Jean
Dawson, unknown, unknown, Maureen Ince, Carol ? and Ann Carruthers.

When the Hirst North School changed its name in 1972, these were three of the lads who played for the school team, setting a record that could never be broken by ending the season as League Champions, Challenge Cup winners and County Cup winners. Seen at Hirst Welfare (flats in back ground are now demolished) on left David Riches, Steven Nichol and Billy Bennett (son of the late Ronnie).

'As headteacher at the North School, I felt some of my successes included: having the outdoor toilets in the far corner of the yard pulled down and indoor toilets provided (1968); and I was quite proud of what I thought was the sensational effect the newly-introduced school uniform had on the appearance and ethos of the school. Another highlight in 1966 was putting on an exhibition of Charlton memorabilia after the World Cup. Jack Charlton was great with all his stuff – he threw England shirts, international caps and World Cup replicas into a suitcase, saying: "Here ye are, tek as much as ye like!"'

Nat Graham

With the advent of comprehensive education in the 1970s, the name of Hirst North School disappeared to be replaced by Milburn First and Cavendish First, although one building did house 'Hirst North Nursery'. The old buildings were finally demolished in 1997 and the pupils moved over the road to a purpose-built school. But the traditional and well-respected name of 'Hirst North' was rejected by the new school governors in favour of 'Central', the name already associated with a nearby workingmen's club.

Hirst South School

SOUTH SCHOOLS, HIRST, ASHINGTON. 1793.

Ashington New Hirst South Council School took its first intake of pupils on 12th October 1908. It was then split into three: a Boys' School with 450 pupils under the Headship of Mr Harrison Clough; a Girls' School with 351 pupils led by Miss Isabella Matthewson; and a Mixed Infants and Junior of 171 boys and 153 girls whose teachers included Isabella Burgess and Jessie Sproat. Christina Haynes was appointed Headmistress in June 1912.

Only six months after opening, the school had to be closed for three weeks because of a measles' epidemic. Some other revealing items, collated by ex-pupil Colin Wanless, show how Hirst schools were directly affected by what was happening in the community in those days.

22/5/1911   School closed this afternoon – a circus is visiting town.
2/2/1912   Very stormy morning. Teachers and pupils arrived with wet feet, so did not mark the register, but sent children home.
12/2/1913   School closed at 12 noon to allow children to see aeroplane.
28/8/1913   School closed at 2.05 pm owing to official opening of New East School.
31/10/1916 School closed. The premises have been requisitioned by the Military.
4/6/1917   We resume occupation of South School.
25/1/1918   A very poor attendance again. (Owing to) the necessity for children to seek and stand waiting for food supplies.
3/7/1918   Almost half the school absent through Spanish Influenza.
26/8/1918   Class V has 84 children with one teacher.
30/6/1919   The Men have laid the Pit idle till Wednesday. The 'Mob' tried to shut the school. (Note: this was the day set aside for 'Peace Celebrations'.)
31/8/1921   Mr Clough terminated his duties as Headmaster.

Hirst South School Morris Dancers, 1948
by Colin Wanless

Among my many happy memories of the Hirst South School is a special one of being a member of the Morris Dancers under the guidance of our class teacher, Mr Andy Foreman, between 1945-48. It was then a tradition of the school for Mr Foreman to teach the same group of boys (3A-4A) while alternating with Mr Bill Armstrong. We were introduced to the dance through Physical Training lessons.

Having learnt a few basic steps, we were then taught hand and arm movements. Two teams of eight were chosen which became the school's A and B team. We were then provided with blue PT shorts and bells sewn on to strips of material to wear below the knee. We were asked to purchase our own white shirts, two large white handkerchiefs, and a pair of sandshoes. Music was provided by a gramophone record of *Country Garden* and, after been taught a 'Beanstick' dance, we were ready to face the outside world of competition.

It was a big event the day that pupils, parents and teachers went by bus to Newcastle City Hall to support our team. Everyone was thrilled when we took First Prize, but we owed our success to Andrew Crozier Foreman. Andy had commenced his duties at the Hirst South School in September 1924 at the age of twenty-one. He was a founder member of the Ashington Pitmen Painters' Group.

The team featured in our photo taken in the school yard is, back row: Robert Thompson (became an Art teacher), Danny Cole (from the well-known Cole family of councillors), Bobby Whitehead (played football for Newcastle United), Leslie Barron, Tom Lashley. Seated: Bob Batey, Derek Wrightson, Brian Welsh and myself, Colin Wanless. Later that same year, Bob Thompson passed the scholarship and went to Bedlington Grammar School, while Derek Wrightson and I also passed and went to Morpeth King Edward VI Grammar School.

Andy Foreman is seen here top left of Hirst South's Boys' choir from 1949. Back row: George Young, Tommy Baird, Colin Trotter, Michael Gray, Spencer Wilkins, Robert Churchill, Kenny Wood, Gordon Watson, Sid Swinhoe, Ronnie Dodds, Ken Wharrier, Mr K. Humble (Head). Second back row: Ronnie Routledge, John Hall, Brian Stoddart, Harvey Nelson, Billy Thompson, Terry Lennox, Tom Hedley, Michael Harn, Brian Laseby, Alan Mullin. Second front row: Bob Morton, David Glass, Brian Dodds, James Schofield, Brian Davison, Miss Audrey Stimpson (accompanist at Central Hall as well as choir leader), Alan Lisle, Trevor Richell, Ken Thornton, Joe Lashley, Billy Robinson, Alan Ruddick. Front row: David Thompson, David Temperley, Alan Simmons (a future Head at Newbiggin Middle School), Billy Brown, Ernie Littlewood, Charlie Grint, Ken Routledge and Trevor Noble.

These were teachers staffing Hirst South Girls School in 1945. Back row: Mrs Thompson, Miss Henderson, Miss Isobel Sanderson (Head), Mrs Dunn. Front row: Miss Alder, Miss McLean and (possibly) Mrs Pearson.

Hirst South Girls, 1946. Back row: Miss Henderson, Mary Sweet, Jean Allison, Elizabeth Owen, Jean Gillis, Doreen Nichol, Isobel Locket, Shirley Maddison, Ruth Morton, Joan Oliver, Miss Sanderson (Head). Middle row: Mary Perry, Margaret Main, Sylvia Kennedy, Stephanie Davison, Margaret Brotherick, Elizabeth Jewers, Sheila Malone, Jean Matthewson, Joan Mullin, Alice Johnson, Mary Leslie. Front row: Margaret Routledge, Margaret Dryden, June Simpson, Jean Leddy, Audrey Corbett, Ann Talbot, Ethel Morris, Elizabeth Turnbull, Joyce Nelson, Betty Agan and Shirley Burns.

Hirst Villa Juniors, 1950. These lads trained at Hirst South School while playing in the East Northumberland Junior League. Back row: Bob Middlemiss, Donald Guy, Ken Key, Walter Harmison, Michael Kirkup, Jim and Alan Longstaff, Louis Rogers (trainer). Front row: Joe Parry, Tom Liddle, Ernie Eastlake, Ron McLain and Jackie Robinson. Sadly, five of the above have passed away.

Hirst South Boys' Choir, 1951, gave a performance at the Central Hall on the occasion of a presentation to Jackie Milburn after his feat in scoring both girls in the FA Cup Final against Blackpool. Handing over a weekend case is Council Chairman A.T. Rogers. Seated on left are two of Milburn's team-mates Jack Fairbrother and George Robledo. Leaning forward on left is Normanton Barron. The two men on bottom right are Councillor Brotherton and George Tate, a council official. Bobby Gray JP is on right in centre. The choir are seated in back row.

Hirst South Girls, 1953. Back row: Brenda Locker, Joan Wallace, Carol Parkes, Linda Moffatt, Kitty Brubaker, Brenda Self, Margaret Bell, Mona Burns, Maureen McCartney, Norah Graham. Second back row: Vivian Gorman, Joan Elsdon, Margaret Reay, Brenda Crawford, Mary Bourne, Sheila Robertson, Pamela Straughan, Christine Sutcliffe, Lynn Sparrow, Coral McGlen. Second front row: Margaret Pike, Gillian Finlay, Maureen Curran, Ann Timpson, Jean Jones, Miss Hedley, Valerie Matthews, Lorna Fenwick, Jennifer Drakesmith, Marjorie Gibbons, Marilyn Lynn. Front row: Phoebe Parker, Bonita Munday, Joyce McCallum, Shirley Cadwallender, Janet Taylor, Elizabeth Main, Jean Foster, Margaret Lawson, Edna Swan and Linda Young.

In 1954 there was a young lad attending Hirst South School who probably never dreamed he would be involved in mining when he left school. But Norman Barron went on to become an electrical engineer at Woodhorn and other local collieries. He has identified some of his schoolmates in this photo of the Hirst South School Choir *circa* 1954 who had carried off most of the trophies from the North of England Music Tournament held that year at Hexham. The music teacher was Nat Graham on the left with headmaster Jack Cutter on right. Back row: ? Baird, then Bernard Allen who went on the mechanical side at Ellington Pit before going to work for Searle's; John Sewell (father Charlie Sewell) was a student apprentice at one time and lived in Hawthorn Road; Billy Hogg who lived in Chestnut Street, went on to the electrical side before emigrating to Canada; Peter Cummings played a bit of cricket, worked as an colliery electrician; Eric Hindmarsh lived at 292 Sycamore Street, his late father Jack played professional football as a full-back and his mother died recently, Eric now lives in Newcastle area; next not named; Michael Elliott of Titchfield Terrace whose father sold Pink Paraffin, still lives local; John Price of No 1 Coronation Terrace, the family moved up into the country past Dyke Neuk. Second back row: ? Newton whose father was a preacher at a little chapel on North Seaton Road, beside Conshie Club; Alan Rowan lived at the bottom of either Maple or Chestnut, he possibly went to London and married an Italian girl; un-named; then Denis Taylor who lived at 25 Richardson Street who went on to the mechanical side at the colliery, now in the publishing business and living in Surrey in a house named 'Wansbeck'; Norman Barron himself who says 'I think that is a cut-down coat I am wearing which my mother made up from my brother's top coat'; Ralph Messenger whose family had a fish and chip shop on Seventh Avenue; Jeff Davis lived above Hill's shop beside Speddings (near the Hipp) went into Fire Brigade and still lives local; Bob Charlton went on to be an electrician at Linton Colliery, lived in Norham Road and married Margaret Nichol of Stakeford, went down to Stevenage to work for BAe but died on his way to work one day aged only forty; Bob Ullock who is also deceased, worked for a time at local ASDA store. Second front row: Billy Brennan possibly lived in Richardson Street; Eddie Armstrong lived three doors up from the Hipp in Coronation Terrace, went to

Art school; Billy Henderson who recently died in Australia; David? Walton possibly lived in Norham Road; Don Wilson on mechanical side at Woodhorn Colliery lived in Rosalind Street; Jetty Turbill whose father Wilf was a policeman, now living in Newbiggin and working in Garden Centre outside Morpeth; David Staines married Anne Pickering of Lynemouth, became quality surveyor and lived in Seventh Avenue; Ian Davison who became electrician at Ashington Pit; and Noel Yellowley who did the same at Lynemouth. Front row: Joe Butters; Ken Thompson?; Reggie Shotton; Bob Shiel lived in Rosalind Street, became electrician at Woodhorn, now works for Citizens Advice Bureau; ? Bewick from Bewick's shop; John Ritchie from Bywell Road who was signed by Stanley Matthews to play football for Port Vale; Hodgson? of East Villas; Terence ?. Norman ends by saying: 'I wonder if there is any significance about a lot of these young singers turning to the electrical trade?'

Hirst South 'Raggle Taggle Gypsies', 1957. The South School was successful in most things artistic. This stemmed from enthusiastic and talented teachers. This little lot were coached by Natty Graham who, according to Frank Fletcher, was 'a tremendous teacher and musician'. This event centred around a song called *The Raggle Taggle Gypsies*. Cast in back row: Doug Wallace, John Pettigrew, Lloyd Bookless, Cliff Wood, Martin Morse, Ronnie Smith, Bobby Butters, Peter Gray. Middle row: Dickie Brewis, Alan Gair, Bob Taylor, Malcolm Hodgson, Lenny Foster, Colin Taylor. Front row: Colin Pearson, Robert Ridley, Frank Fletcher, John Ross, John Tinkler and Charlie Nelson. Frank also says that a large number of these lads formed the backbone of the senior form at Ashington Grammar School when that opened in 1960.

Doug Wallace played football at centre half for the county and was on Newcastle's books as a junior until a serious leg injury put him out of the game completely. He subsequently worked as a policeman in the Sunderland area and is now retired. **John Pettigrew**, an all-round sportsman. After the South School he went to a school in the Newcastle area where he became a first-rate rugby player and cricketer, playing for the County Club before he emigrated to

Canada where he now lives as a doctor. His mother was the secretary at Hirst South Boys School for many, many years. **Lloyd Bookless**, a studious class member who went on to Morpeth Grammar after the eleven-plus exam. Later to Oxbridge universities to do Classics. He most probably succeeded in his quest. Where is he now? **Cliffy Wood**, rather quiet bloke who went on to Morpeth Grammar. His ability at mental arithmetic was amazing and we all knew he would succeed at whatever he set out to do; he worked as a laboratory technician at Newcastle University in the Botany department involved with Biochemistry. After much study and hard work he gained a M.Phil and then a PhD. Now runs his own research lab in the School of Biology with the title of Dr Wood. He is deemed a world authority on how plants make and break down fats and oils. Currently lives in Crawcrook in the Tyne valley. **Martin Morse** (deceased). What a funny guy this fella was – the class jester, full of laughs and a pleasure to be around. Was a member of Ashington's ATC 1110 Squadron. Naturally he joined the RAF and went on to be an Officer and no doubt a gentleman. He sadly died at a relatively young age.

Right: Not a lot of people know that Jackie Milburn was a pilot officer. Well, in honour of him being capped for England in 1948, they made him an honorary officer with the ATC of which he was a member during the Second World War.

Ronnie Smith, another bright lad, always near the top of the class. He moved on to the Luton area at around twelve years of age where he probably did very well. Another where is he now? **Bobby Butters** (deceased). My cousin and a friend; not interested in school but another very bright lad. Worked at Lynemouth Colliery as an apprentice fitter. Through much graft and great ability he went on to become Chief Engineer and subsequently the Superintendent of a shipping line. He worked very hard with a view to an early, long and happy retirement, but unfortunately he died when abroad on one of his many trips. Bobby is sadly missed by many. **Dicky Brewis**, another good footballer who played on well past his sell-by date. (That's what I tell him.) Always into the fashion scene and the first to have a made-to-measure suit in the drape and drainpipe style. As a Tax Inspector, Dickie surely cannot be loved by many, other than perhaps his nearest and dearest. Lives locally at North Seaton and he tells me every time I see him that retirement cannot come soon enough. **Alan Gair**, very funny bloke who had the whole class in stitches. Our daily journey to Blyth Grammar School on the bus was hysterical (often to the annoyance of the public) as we travelled back and forth. Alan worked initially as a clerk at Siggin's Quarry, Newbiggin, and is now the production manager at a factory in Cramlington where he lives. **Bob Taylor**, a very good footballer and all-round sportsman. He captained just about every team he has played for. Went to Birmingham University where he received his blues as the captain of both the football and cricket teams. He played cricket for Ashington Cricket Club, again as captain and scored many runs often in the company of the famous West Indian star Rohan Kanhai. He also excelled at squash, which he still plays to a very high standard even though he is in his fifty-seventh year. Lives locally, currently the Head of English at a private Grammar School in Gosforth. **Malclolm Hodgson**, one of the few in the photo with whom I have had no contact since our days at the South School. Where is he now? **Len Foster**, always good at technical drawing and so it was no surprise that upon leaving school he became a civil engineer working for McAlpine. Has been around the world, involved in the building of high profile, high cost buildings, currently the boss on a site in Saudi Arabia supervising the construction of a multi-million pound palace for a Sheik. He is living in Riyadh but his home in the UK is in Hampshire. Len hopes to retire back in the north east in the not too distant future. **Colin Taylor**, a decent footballer, but the thing I remember most about our school days with Colin was a class visit to Hadrian's Wall. Martin Morse was the proud owner of a home-made plate mince pie. He was the envy of the class and made every effort to ensure we all knew of his super treat. Unfortunately he laid it on the ground whereupon Colin, accidentally (we think), trod directly on to the pie. After a spell with Ashington Council, Colin moved into the accountancy field, where he subsequently qualified. Over thirty years with *Glaxo*, or whatever it is now called, at West Sleekburn, Colin still lives in the Ashington area. **Peter Gray**, a year younger than the rest of the class. One of the very first families to move into brand-new, very posh flats called Alexandra Court. He was a bright lad but, due to illness (appendicitis), he recuperated at the old fever hospital at North Seaton now the location of the Nursery Park Estate; I believe he is now a dentist living and practicing in the South of England

    Colin Pearson, another member of the class with whom I have lost contact since our days at school. However, he came across as a hunting, shooting, fishing type of person. I often went bird nesting with him. In the Three Fields near North Seaton Hall we robbed a tree sparrow's nest with Colin 30 feet in the air on the thinnest of branches with myself frantic below in case we had to scrape him up. Where is he now?

North Seaton Hall had been built by the famous John Dobson in the early 19th century. It was demolished around 1960.

Robert Ridley, at that time the smallest in the class and rather quiet retiring sort of lad. His father was Bob Ridley a barber on Milburn Road who competed with both Ernie Cowe and Jackie Sinclair, all within 150 yards of each another. The amazing thing was that from this very small boy a giant evolved almost overnight from the age of seventeen. He became a strong swimmer and, believe it or not, a lifeguard on Newbiggin Beach. Last heard of living in the Lytham St Annes area. **Frank Fletcher**, living in North Seaton and still taking a great interest in the whereabouts and achievements of my former classmates. I have a vivid memory of my old school mates forty-six years on and still remember clearly every name and face from a class of 48 pupils and what a great time it was. I work in local government (now only part-time at Derwentside) as a consultant on housing conditions. **John Ross**, another rather shy and reserved boy who generally kept a low profile. It was not until his late teens that he came forward to surprise us as a singer, musician and songwriter. He

performed regularly at the *Cellar Club* as a member of the Amazing Beanbag Band. He still performs and writes songs in his leisure time and is currently teaching in the Whitley Bay area where he now lives. **John Tinkler**, always a tall gangly lad who mixed in well with everyone. He became very recognisable in his teens when his resemblance to a member of the Shadows group became apparent. His likeness to Hank Marvin, the lead guitarist, was quite remarkable. He currently works as a plumber for one of his former classmates who is missing from the photo. (Arthur Barker, the energy behind Rickard and Barker, the building firm.) John still lives in the Ashington area. **Charlie Nelson**, a very big lad at school, just short of six feet at eleven years of age. Due to his size he was given a position of importance in the school known as a 'porchy'. It was his job to give the staff at school a period of quiet during their breaks by being the *bouncer* at the entrance to the school. Just prior to moving on to secondary school, he and his family emigrated to Canada. I wonder how he is getting on?

Richardson Street, behind Milburn Road, provided many youngsters for the nearby South School. The original Henry Richardson, after whom the street was named around 1900, was an engineer with the Ashington Coal Company in the late 19th century. The two ladies seen here hoyin' in the coals in the 1930s are Lena Morton on right with her friend Millie Lawther, sister of Will a prominent miners' union man. Lena Morton herself was a defender of human rights and once joined a march down to London protesting against the Means Test.

Hirst East School

An article which appeared in October 1913 of *The Building News* commented on the opening of the new Hirst East School:

'The school was officially opened by Sir Francis Blake, chairman of the Northumberland Education Committee. The buildings form an interesting example of the quadrangle principle and are the first of its kind to be built in the North of England. It provides accommodation for 700 mixed and 362 infant children, and occupies a site of almost two acres. A feature of the arrangement is the shape of the classrooms which have been designed so that the distance between the window walls and the walls opposite has been reduced to 21ft thus ensuring considerably more light to the back rows of desks than is afforded in the earlier types of classroom. The necessary teachers' rooms are provided with lavatory and WC accommodation adjoining each room. The buildings have been erected with red pressed facing bricks and covered with Westmorland green slates. The school was designed by, and carried out, under the supervision of Mr G. Topham Forest; Mr J.P. Bell of Newbiggin acted as clerk of works.'

Note: As a tribute to the work done by the Education chairman Sir Francis Blake, all Northumberland schools competed in soccer for the 'Blake Cup', and it was fitting that the name of Hirst East School figured more prominently than any other among the list of proud winners.

Hirst East Boys, 1935/36. One of the most successful Hirst East football teams won the Northumberland and Durham School's Cup in 1936. Back row: Harry Elcott, Mr Jim Wood, Jacques, Thorburn, Harry Freeman, 'Cappy' Mason, Archie Nichol (with ball), Mr Jack Denton (Head), Harry Harle. Seated: Billy Paxton, John Pratt, Harry Burrell, Bobby York and Johnson.

Hirst East Boys, 1937/38. The previous team won many accolades but this squad excelled them. Back row: teacher Jim Wood who became Head at Newbiggin Secondary, Bill Thirtle, Cyril Bird, Bob Jacques, Reddy Rider, Jim Harle, Bill Paxton, Mr Garbutt, Mr Ford. Front row: Dickie Freeman, Tommy Mackie, Albert Johnson, Wor Jackie Milburn and his cousin Jimmy Milburn.

Hirst East Boys, 1946. Back row: Tom Sheill, Malcolm Chambers, Norman Watson, Peter Ford, Bobby Davison, Joe Bowden, Brian Blair, Sid Hutton, Alan Crate, Lance Parkin, Gordon Ray, Joe Hall, George McPherson. Middle row: Mr Roy Paterson, Desmond Watson, John Brotherton, John Stephenson, Joey Emery, Maty Taylor, John Devon, Bill Scott, Ray McGee, unknown, Bill Southern, Ken Rickaby, Terry Carter, Melvyn Wright. Front row: Jackie Robinson, Brian Hesp, Sid Fisher, Wilf Davison, Tommy Dodds, Alan Roughead, Jackie Lightley, Ken Key, Bill Bowden, John Rutherford, Ronnie Leatham, Bob Bartle, Les McGowan and Brian Sanderson.

Hirst East football team at Portland Park 1949. Back row: Mr Hudson, Bill Southern, Brian Hesp, Eric 'Spike' Newman, Ray Bell, Alan Taylor, John Hale and Mr Liddle. Front row: Jackie Winn, Andy Purvis, Jimmy Jackson, Sid Hutton and Joe Green.

Hirst East Boys, 1949. Back row: Charlie Robinson, Billy Bell, Arthur Harper, Peter Bell, Alan Oliver, Jimmy Collins, Derek Fowler, Ernie Griffiths, Tom Yorke, Mr Harry Finlay. Middle row: Dickie Dewar, Bill Hudspeth, Ron Patterson, John Hope, Jim Anderson, Donny Poole, Tom Anderson, Ron Curry, S. Parkin, Frank Snaith, Jackie Swalwell. Front row: Ken Latimer, Brian Yeardon, Ken Lillico, Charlie Cole, Jack Phillips, Chris Henderson, Bob Roberts, G. Williams. In front: Kenny Yeats and Alan Wren.

Marionettes at Hirst East, 1949. With guidance from Mr Douglas and Mr Les Brownrigg, these lads made their own puppets and put on a show for the whole school. One member of the cast, Harold Drinkwater, was not present for this photo which shows back row: unknown, Ron Little, Brian Fenwick, Ed Pearson, unknown, Alan Scott, Alan Blevins. Front row: Brian Hall, Brian Bennett, Alan Wren, Malcolm Scott, Alan Ayre, Mr Douglas and Mr Brownrigg, David Wrightson, Tommy Owen, Tom Morse and Eric Dunnett.

The Gold Watches presented to

JACK MILBURN
NEWCASTLE UNITED F.C.
CAPPED FOR ENGLAND 1948

Chronicle & Journal Photographs

JAMES JACKSON
ENGLISH SCHOOLBOY
INTERNATIONAL 1949

by the
People of Ashington

Hirst East School had two of their ex-pupils honoured for being awarded England caps in the same 1948/49 season. It was football fanatic George Cave who suggested that the town should recognise the amazing feat of young Jimmy Jackson and Jackie Milburn by presenting the pair with gold watches from Carr's the Jeweller. The presentation took place at the Hirst Premier Club.

Hirst East Boys, 1950. Back row: Jackie Scott, Bob Carr, Bob Brown, Alan Blair, unknown, Eric Dunnett, Albert 'Billy' Gardner. Middle row: Mr Thain, Neil Patterson, Brian Hall, Ronnie Curry, Billy Robson, Alan Belvins, Bob Clark, Norman Lowther, Brian Lowes, Tom Morse, Ray 'Chick' Henderson. Front row: Lisle Brown, unknown, Tommy Winn, George Barkwell, Ernie Adey, George Mason, Gerald O'Brien (perhaps adopted or fostered by the Dawson family), Ron Cook, Colin Tewart. In front: Jim Southern, Alan Robson and Chris Parmley.

Hirst East Girls, 1953. Back row: Gloria Graham, Edna Johnson, Eileen McKenna, Margaret Grieves, Dorothy Charlton, Isa McCready, Jean Humphreys, Doris Erskine, Jean Weldon, Helen McDonald, Joan Glynn, Joyce Paxton. Middle row: Maureen Nesbit, Marjorie Smith, Winnie Gilroy, Miss Coils, Glynis Rossiter, June Fairweather, Elsie Redfearn, Jennie Mann. Front row: Winnie Gallon, Mildred Thompson, Margaret Main, Margaret Yearham, Madelaine Donald, Margaret Dunn and Veronica Hewitt.

Hirst East Girls, 1954. Front row: Edna Allison, Beryl Carlisle, Ida Johnson, Marion Lillico, Betty Bullows, Olive Patterson, Eleanor Adamson, Pat Patterson, Jessie Short. Middle row: Miss Rowell, Pat Orkney, Pat Longstaff, Lottie Murray, Maureen Bowman, Ann Heard, Lilian Greener, Margaret Phillips, Mrs Hetherington. Back row: Margaret Norris, Janey Baker, Laura Bell, Carol Adey, Eunice Pile, Ina Thompson and Betty Smith.

Many of the Hirst girls obtained employment at one of the factories on the Jubilee Trading Estate. Reyrolles factory had been built behind North Seaton Road in the early years of the Second World War where it turned out top secret bomb sights. Girls on this 1951 photo include: B. Partis, T. Nesbitt, B. Burton, Ivy Batch and Grace Harrison (née Field) who is kneeling in centre.

Hirst Park School

With three schools at Hirst named North, South and East, it was inevitable that the next to be built would have some geographical connotations. And so it was that the Hirst Central School (later Hirst Park Modern) opened in 1928 catering for boys and girls between the ages of 11 and 14. Leading the girls' school was Miss Gordon, while Mr Charles Hemmingway was Head of boys. The 'Park' was modern in every way, even to the extent of having flush toilets. From the beginning, a great emphasis was placed on school pride and discipline; children wore uniforms, which up till then had been used solely by Grammar Schools. It was the ethos of the time that much of the teaching at this particular type of secondary school would have a leaning towards the practical with adequate workshops and domestic science rooms made available in the new buildings.

Miss Mildred Watson joined the teaching staff at Hirst Park as a 20-year-old in 1936. She recalls:

'It was a big school and the classes were streamed; my first class was a 'C' group. I was very glad going into the Staff Room that first day to find people who had been at Morpeth High School with me. Miss Auty was Head then and Miss Joisce had all the 'A' forms for PE. The classrooms were built around a grassed courtyard with open arches to corridors, making it very draughty. These were filled in much later and what a difference that made to warmth. We took children from the South and North schools, and there was a variety of talent. We had some very good children.

These are the Park School Girls teachers around 1945: Included: Mildred Watson, Marjorie ?, Miss Cole, Ann Perry, Shirley Wilkinson, Lesley Miles, Miss Ingram, Miss Autey (Head), Hilda Easton, Ethel Youngs and Anna Watson.

'Netball took place in the school yard as the field at Hirst Park was full of ashes and rubbish. When I was doing Local History I took classes to meetings in the Council Chambers. Once the chairman said the girls could ask questions and, to my amazement, one girl stood up and said: "We can't play Rounders on the Park field because of all the glass. Do you think the Council can do something about it?" And they did. The workmen came very shortly afterwards and levelled it.

'The school closed at the outbreak of the Second World War in September 1939 and we remained closed for about six weeks. That's when it became an ARP point, and we staff had to fill sandbags.

'Later in the 1950s and '60s I conducted choirs of Hirst Park girls at the Central Hall and it was always packed with children upstairs and guests downstairs. The first opera we did was *Hiawatha* in 1953, and Sheila Armstrong was only eleven when she took the part of Hansel in *Hansel and Gretel* in 1954. Dorothy Hall was Gretel, and Joyce Williams played the witch. But we had lots of good girls at Hirst Park, many of whom still keep in touch. I enjoyed the forty years I spent there.'

Sheila Armstrong is on the left playing Hansel with Dorothy Hall (Gretel) and Joyce Williams (Witch).

Sheila Armstrong was one of Hirst Park's first girls to make the grade as an opera singer; another who followed in her footsteps a couple of years later was Maureen Williams who came back to Ashington in 1994 to sing in *Fell 'em Doon – Birth of a Pit Village*. The third of Ashington's opera singers, Janice Cairns was the daughter of Roly who for many years ran the Handyman's Shop on North Seaton Road.

Harry Harle is featured with the Hirst East football team of 1936 and his wife-to-be Peggy Cole is seen with this squad of girls at the Park School in the late 1930s. Peggy says that these girls left school without any prospect of getting a job. She said: 'Some of us went to train at the Thomas Knight Memorial Hospital in Blyth where we learnt all sorts of things.' Back row: Doris Peart, Emily Madigan, Peggy Prime, Millie Besford, Jean Baird. Front row: Mary Gascoigne, Gwen Potts and Peggy Harle (née Cole).

Hirst Park Girls netball, 1943. Jessie Jeffrey says that she is with girls standing in front of the air-raid shelter in the school yard during the Second World War. She recalls that her teachers were: Miss Elliott for PE, Miss Mildred Watson taught History and Music, Miss Wilkinson was Maths, Miss Youngs Needlework, and Miss Lawson taught French. Girls from back: Jean Morell, Isobel Railston, unknown, Parmley. Middle row: Jessie Jeffrey, Miriam Harper, unknown, Hilda Parmley, Sylvia Clough. Front row: unknown, Thelma Mather and Millie Duff.

Hirst Park football team, 1945. Back row: Charlie Hemmingway (Headmaster), Tom Liddle, 'Sam' Robinson, Murdie, Christie, Alan White and Mr Boucher whose parents had Boucher's post office. Seated: Les Brannigan, Bill 'Skinty' Bowden, Bob Dodds, Cyril Beddard, Girling Jamieson. On ground: Cairns and Burt.

Larry Bell's Boys Club, 1949. This squad included many lads from the East and Park schools. Back row: Alec Freebody, unknown, Mr Alec Winn, Alan Young, Matty Taylor, Alan Robson, Billy Merryweather, Les Renwick, Joe Green, Jackie Winn, unknown. Front row: Les Robson, Tom Liddle, Tom Wear, Bill Robson, Cyril Beddard and Ray Bell.

Hirst Park Girl Guides, 1950. Back row: Jean Gillis, Jean Allison, Mary Bell, Joan Denwood, Joyce Lord, Alice Bullimore. Second back row: Margaret Hindhaugh, Muriel Bell, Audrey Ferguson, Edna Chapman, Lavinia Cummings, Margaret Dodds, Edith Glass, Margaret Brotherick, Miss Wilkinson. Second front row: June Swan, Mary Perry, Margaret Routledge, Audrey Corbett, Dorothy Rossiter, Jean Leddy. Front row: Doreen Sands, Irene Tewart, Ann Waddle, Marina Hamilton and Joan Bell.

Hirst Park Girls' Choir, 1950. Back row: Dorothy Rossiter, Dorothy Wilkinson, Margaret Routledge, Ann Wade, Vera Mordue, Lily Rump, Margaret Cooper, Mary Leslie, Rachael Sampson, Maureen Agan. Middle row: Betty Renner, Joan Laws, Bernadene Reed, Mary Bell, Jean Gillis, Margaret Younger, Lexa Curtis, Edna Chapman, Jean Allison, Betty Grieves, Alice Johnson. Front row: Edith Glass, Joyce Nelson, Betty Agan, Jean Kenyon, Shirley Mitchelson, Elsie Garrett, Joan Littlewood, Mary Perry, Sylvia Lawrence, Jean Leddy and Joan Denwood. Music teacher and conductor, Miss Mildred Watson is on right.

Hirst Park Boys, 1951. Back row: Micky Cummings, John Warren, Tom Herron, Charlie Wright, John Arthur, David Baird, Bobby Cutting, Colin Chapman. Middle row: Dougie Morris, Alan Messenger, Ken Turnbull, Dick McGrath, Derek Bowman, Jack Penman, Brian Critchlow, Bob Sturgeon. Front row: Derek Woof, Joe Davison, Roy Soppitt, Maurice Irwin, Alan Caldwell, Mr Tom Thompson (former POW), Clive Atkinson, Steve Davison, Ronnie Parmley, David Key and Richard Storey.

Hirst Park football team, 1952. It was very much a Sunderland v Newcastle presentation at the Park School in 1952. They had asked Jackie Milburn to present the trophies, but that fell through. Then someone suggested Jimmy Adamson, Burnley's stylish half-back. And so it was that Jimmy, who later managed Sunderland, handed out awards to a future Newcastle United player, Bobby Whitehead, and a future Sunderland goalkeeper, Ronnie Routledge.

From left: teacher Sam Hart, Jimmy Adamson, Bobby Whitehead, Ken Millican, Les Barron, Ron Routledge, Brian Bennett, Walter Lavery, Micky Cummings. In front: Jim Bartholomew, Tom Herron, Bob Mavin, Alan Smith and Harry Dodd.

Hirst Park Girl Guides, 1953. Back row: unknown, Ann Laws, Elsie Nichol, Mary Lou Saunders, Josephine ?, Elisie Goodsell, Lillian Clinton, Margaret Crate, Florence ?, Ellen ?, Shirley Crooks. Middle row: unknown, Jean Derbyshire, unknown, Sheila Curran, unknown, Ann Reaveley, unknown, Maureen Hill, Brenda Flawell, Freda ?, Jean Jamieson. Front row: unknown, Sheila Skinner, unknown, Dorothy ?, unknown, Miss Wilkinson, Joan ?, Stephanie ?, Doreen Denwood, Elizabeth Steel and unknown.

Hirst Park Boys, 1955. They will now be in their 60s but back then their life lay ahead of them. Back row: Billy Hornsby, Arthur Bolton, John Robson, Billy Robinson, Ray Dunning, Brian Jameson, Tony Mercel, Jack Fox, Billy Allport, unknown. Middle row: Johnny Gordon, Bill Brian, Terry Yearham, Michael Ullock, Bill Harris, Harry Stobbart, Malcolm Walsh, Henry Murphy, Richard Johnson, Ernie Johnson. Front row: Keith Johnson, John Jennings, Dennis Lister, Tom Hallowell, Ray Banks, Mr Tommy Thompson, Derek Oxberry, John Bullough, Derek Lister, Alan Davison and Bill Proctor.

Hirst Park Sports Day, 1956. In fact it was held at the Hirst Welfare. Cissie Charlton, front centre made sure the event went off with high jinx. Ladies from left (most of whom were from Beatrice Street) were: unknown, Mrs Dixon, Cissie, Mrs Cameron, Lizzie Furness and Mrs Wilkinson. Some Park School pupils at the back are blatantly smoking. They include Walter Lavery in cap, Cath Thompson, Billy Merryweather and ginger Tommy Morton; most of these lived in Pont Street.

Hirst Park football team, 1957. This was the team beaten 3-1 by Stephenson School, Wallsend, in the final of the Blake Cup. Back row: Colin Furness, Billy Reavley, Tommy Randall, Brian Robinson, Eric Turnbull, Bobby Sweet. Front row: George Brotherick, John Cummings, Matty Poole, Eddie Bircham and John Hall.

Hirst Park Girls in London, 1958. This group went with two teachers – Miss Watson and Miss Youngs – seen back left. The party were shown around Westminster by the then MP for Morpeth, Will Owen, front centre.

A reunion of some Hirst Park Girls took place in the year 2000. It was decided to make their teacher, Miss Mildred Watson, the guest of honour. Mildred brought along her scrapbook to show the girls. Back row: Doreen Denwood, Betty McGinley, Joyce Lord, Elizabeth Drysdale, Freda Oliver, Jean Allison, Joan Denwood. Seated: Doreen Wilson, Miss Watson and Marie Aitchieson, at her house in Green Lane.

This Ashington YMCA junior squad played in the late 1940s. Back row: trainer Jack Simmons, Ray Logan, Gordon Richardson, unknown, 'Pop' Anderson, Ken Stephen, 'Hacker' Robins. Front row: Gus Wilson, unknown, Ernie Charlton, Ron Talbot, Sammy Robinson and Lol Weddle.

Although not technically in the Hirst, St Aidan's RC School provided education for many pupils who came from the colliery rows of Maple, Sycamore and Chestnut etc. This class of 1950 was full of Hirst children. They include: Ronnie Knox, Peter Heard, Aaron Johnson, Ronnie McMillan, Jimmy Southern, Joe Wilks, George Scott, Robert Guy, Ivan Clark, Joe Conroy, Bill Smith, Arthur Self, Joe Cain and Paddy Brennan. Some of the girls include: Theresa Clark, Ann Barton, Doreen Hanson, Pat Humphreys, Freda Lang, Delia Hunt, Ina Buller and Pat Coates.

Another St Aidan's class from 1950. Back row: Matty Hall, Jimmy Bonner, Alan Dixon, Phil Sikkink, George Mitchelson, Ed White, Joe Ball, John Coates, Basil Robertson, Raymond Gray, Edmund Redford. Middle row: Ann Langan, Margaret Maxwell, Brenda Wilkinson, Shirley Barber, Selina Brennan, Theresa Clark, Edna Savage, Margaret Ibbotson. Front row: Margaret Goldsberry, Mary Cooney, Betty Tait, Audrey Rainbow, Margaret Scott, Mr Kingston, Rosina Scott, Rose Stokoe, Veronica Rowley, Irene Smith and Ann Angus.

In the 1970s, a new senior school for Catholic children was built down Moorhouse Lane, called St Benedict's. Yet another Catholic School sprang up on the North Seaton Road Estate in 1974 – this was for infant pupils and called St Aidan's First School, seen here being visited by Mrs Mazzolini soon after the school opened.

Ashington Tech College

Building work began on the new Technical College in the early-1950s, as seen here.

A Mining School was opened in Darnley Road in 1930 to cater for students involved in the mining industry. It went under the grand title of the Ashington Welfare Educational Institute, a name that was dropped when the 1944 Education Act was passed. It then became the Ashington County College and Mining School. New courses started up: Bakery and Confectionery drew in an extra 30 students, while Motor Engineering attracted another 45. The principal of the college, Mr Pulford, saw his salary rise to £725 in 1945.

The nationalisation of the coal industry in 1947 resulted in the absorption of Ashington Coal Company by the National Coal Board. The ACC ties were finally severed by a letter from the Education Committee on 14th April 1947, noting that: 'We are very grateful to the Ashington Coal Company for the role they have played in Education in the Ashington area.' At the same time, a new County Plan for Education had been drawn up based on three points:

1. A Technical College for boys and girls to be built at Ashington (Hirst) as part of the extension of the Mining School as a Technical College.
2. A County College for boys to be established at Ashington (Hirst) for day students only.
3. The existing Mining School to be remodelled as a Technical College with departments for Industrial Art, Design and Crafts.

The buildings for all the above were to be 'Provided on the existing site plus additional areas of approximately 17 acres and 18 acres to the south and south-west of the present site.' That site, in effect, was a piece of land affectionately known as Wembley Field, so called to coincide with the building of Wembley Stadium around 1923.

The Pont Street Mob

by Jimmy Main

I recall when foot-running was very popular, especially by the mob in Pont Street at the Hirst. When these running events occurred the whole street would turn out. Pont Street housed a number of large families who considered themselves as better than average runners. A few names come to mind, such as Ronnie Armstrong, a couple of the Merryweather boys, the Halls, who would gamble on the result of the races (which were always handicapped). The races tended to be a closed shop except to the inhabitants of Pont Street which tended to be a tough place those days – you just did not venture down there without an invitation.

Here are some Pont Street lads having a pint at the White Elephant in the early 1950s. On left Walter 'Skinny' Harmison, Johnny 'Snakey' Nixon, Eric 'Tooter' Scott and Bobby Lisle. The Harmison clan have certainly made a name for themselves with regard to sport in the area. Steve Harmison is currently playing cricket for Durham and England while others from the same family are represented on Ashington football team.

The South Primary School was a single-storey building, with all classrooms leading off the main hall. The caretaker was a Mr Longstaff. Most of the teachers at the South in the 1940s were women, as the male teachers were at war. Although the women teachers did their best for us boys, they did not have the control that male teachers tend to project. One such teacher was a Miss Burgess, a dear old soul in her sixties. I suppose everyone liked her, but she lacked the control needed for unruly boys. And then there was Miss Clarkson. Her form of punishment was to raise your pants and smack the top of your leg – big deal. It was not until I reached the top form that I had a male teacher.

Mr Armstrong was the first, although very strict, I thought the world of him. He was very interested in professional foot-races, and even more so when he knew that my brother Norman (Pentland) was also a professional foot-runner. So we had a common bond to share, hence my adulation for this teacher. In later years, I recall when I 'had a go' for the Morpeth Olympic Games in the 1950s. He came to see me before the start of the heats to ask if I was worth a bet. Not wanting to spoil the betting, I introduced him to Norman who placed a bet on for him. I finished runner-up in the final.

My first day at the Park School was a bit traumatic. The older boys of the school always tried to intimidate the new intake by a type of torture called the 'stocks', a matter of placing the unfortunate boys arms through the iron railings which were held by some cohort of the boy doing the bullying. However, I escaped stocks because of my running prowess, I was too speedy

Jimmy Main on left, and his elder brother, Norman, were both crack sprinters – they emigrated to Australia.

for them to catch me. As time went by, the older boys forgot who they had initiated and who they had not, and I was not going to volunteer that I had escaped the initiation test.

The names of some of my teachers I remember were: Messrs Hart, Stephenson, Graham, Ellis, McHugh, Willis, Bell, and two women teachers by the name of Miss Todd and Miss Chambers; the Headmaster was called Charlie Hemmingway.

School football was very strong those days. I played right-half for the school team. Another member of the school team was Jackie Charlton (seen here aged 21 at Leeds United). Even those days Jackie played centre-half. The local derby was always against the Hirst East School. Their most notable player was Jim (Chinky) Jackson who went on to play for England Schoolboys. I believe Jimmy played professionally for one of the lower division teams near London, possibly Aldershot. Percy Armstrong from the Park School also played as a schoolboy international.

Sid Hutton and Jimmy Jackson played in this Hirst East team in 1947; they are seated 3rd left and 2nd right.

I was good enough at football to get a trial for East Northumberland. However, I was up against players like Jackson and Sid Hutton who went on to play for Newcastle. As the competition for a place was very strong, I did not get a place in the team. I suppose my forte was athletics where I won both the Junior and Senior Athletics Championship Medal.

Mr Ellis was our woodwork teacher and had little patience. He was also the master in charge of Blake House. Mr Ellis was renowned for throwing pieces of wood the length of the woodwork room into the scrap box. I never could to this day plane a piece of wood level.

Mr McHugh took Geography which I considered a boring subject. Mr Hart took Maths. He stood well over six foot in height: a very intimidating master. Mr Stephenson was our sports

Jimmy Main on right with Tom Thornton and Bill Coates.

master and played football until he got his leg broken. Mr Willis was our English teacher (ex-RAF). Mr Bell was the Art teacher. The Headmaster of the school was Mr Hemingway or Old Charlie as us kids knew him. Charlie was always dressed in flowing black robes. He was a short plumpish man with a strong baritone voice. Old Charlie was known to have a bit of a temper but despite this he was well liked.

The school used corporal punishment to maintain law and order. This was in the shape of a piece of leather belt some eighteen inches in length and about a quarter inch in thickness. The belt was located in the Headmaster's office along with the punishment book. For a misdemeanour requiring the belt, the offending boy would go up to the Headmaster's office. He would then knock on the door. Charlie's voice would call out 'enter', and the boy would then politely ask for the book and belt. Charlie would then point with open hand and say 'with pleasure'.

At the end of each school year, we assembled in the main hall to await the arrival of the Headmaster (he was always late) and on his arrival we would all sing 'Charlie is me Darling' at the top of our voices. Charlie beamed with approval then took us through a number of songs, being a baritone of some repute. This was followed by speeches, saying goodbye to the senior boys and wishing them well in their future life. I must add that the headmaster was a big Gilbert and Sullivan fan and many photographs ordained the school walls of the various casts of the *Mikado, Pirates of Penzance* and *The Gondoliers*.

Many of the productions of the Ashington Operatic Society, of which Charles Hemmingway was a keen member, were performed in the Arcade Hall. The Hall is seen here decked out with rather uncomfortable-looking chairs. But it was as a dancehall that the Arcade will be long remembered. The Arcade with Eric Nichol and Connie Allsopp on vocals, and Joe Gray's Arcadian danceband, delighted thousands of dancers throughout the 1940s and '50s.

SECTION FIVE

HIRST AT WAR ... AND PEACE

The North School Corner was painted by Oliver Kilbourn. Wartime in Hirst around 1941 meant 'blackout' as cars and buses crept around the main roads after dark with a minimum of light coming from a slit in the brown paper that covered each headlamp. There were accidents galore as vehicles mounted unlit pavements. A nightly highlight – excuse the pun – was when the Pavilion Cinema (the Piv) came out at ten o'clock and the second house patrons emerged into a pitch-black Milburn Road. It was then that the humble torch, or flashlight as it was called then, came into its own. (That is if you were able to obtain batteries for it.) It was a weird sight to see about two hundred narrow beams of light focused on the pavement as the 'canny folk of Horst Ashin'ton' walked past the high wooden railings of Hirst North School, negotiated the corner into 2nd Avenue, and then peeled off into their homes at Sycamore, Maple or Chestnut streets.

The Pavilion Theatre featured live shows right up to the onset of World War Two. Here are four chorus girls who danced in the 1937 production of *Goodnight Vienna* at the Piv. From left: Gladys Boutland, Jean Ledgerwood, Nellie Potts and Laura Newman.

On leaving the Piv the lucky ones who had money to spare, instead of going straight home, headed for their favourite chip shop. And at Hirst you had a great selection. There was the choice of two in 1st Avenue: Browns and Meg Dawsons. Brown had the shop at the top of Poplar Street, while Meg was at the bottom of 1st Avenue odd-numbered Maple Street. The most popular order was 'a fish and a pennorth, please, Meg, and plenty of scranshuns.' And that might set you back all of a tanner (sixpence or two and a half new pence). Other fish shops in that close vicinity included: Drinkwater's, Bailey's and Allison's. But you only had to go down a block or to the east side of Hawthorn Road, to find many more.

From the outset of the Second World War, Ashington and Hirst were completely mobilised. Each part of the town was split into sections for purposes of civil detence; ARP headquarters sprung up all over, based mainly at local schools.

The *Ashington Post* of 4th September 1940 carried these caricatures (opposite page) of local men who held positions of responsibility with regard to Civil Defence.

No 1 was George W. Tate who was the chief sanitary inspector for Ashington Council at the time. His new wartime position was as Mortuary Superintendent.

No 2 was the Roman Catholic priest at St Aidan's, Father John Patrick Mullarkey. The priest's new role was to be as Deputy Chief Warden.

No 3 was Alf Shepherd who owned the Princess Ballroom. Also a councillor, Alf was to be the Billeting Officer responsible for finding accommodation for the many troops who came into the town.

No 4 Arthur Wilkinson, was also a councillor. The Wilkinsons owned a shop and printing works in the town. Arthur was to be a Head Warden.

No 5 was another Head Warden, Peter McMeekin, who became manager at Boots the Chemist on Station Road; his son of the same name later had a dental practice in Laburnum Terrace.

In 1940, because of paper shortage, and owing to wartime restrictions, the pages of the *Ashington Advertiser* were no more than an A3 sheet folded in half. The front page was almost completely taken up with an illustrated advert from F.R. Little, an electrical goods dealer in North Seaton Road, while optician S. Aaron pleaded with the 'Many thousands suffering from eye strain caused through Black-Out Darkness' to have their eyes tested at 37a Station Road.

The front inside page was mainly left over to advertising Ashington's five cinemas. *Pinocchio* was showing at the Wallaw in the week commencing 28th October 1940, prices Adult Stalls 7d, Circle 10d; Child Stalls 4d, Circle 6d. On the opposite page was the programme at the Dog Stadium where the best dog at the time was Cosa Maite, a record-breaking animal.

In the same edition (1940) Ashington Football Club fielded an interesting team that included English international Stan Mortensen as well as Tommy McLain who went on to play for Sunderland. In fact, most of this squad commanded places at clubs in the Football League: Tapken, John Hindmarsh, Bell, McLain, Briggs, Daglish, Dobson, Thompson, Bobby Farrington, McIntosh, Stan Mortensen, Watty Thornton and Len Hays. During the war, because of travel restrictions, players who were in the services were given permission to play for whatever team was nearest to where they were billeted, and that is why Ashington had the pick of the some of the best players in the country.

Tom McLain began work in the Welfare Department of Ashington Colliery. He played for Sunderland soon after being demobbed from the Army after the war.

John Hindmarsh played for Sheffield United, Notts County and Burnley.

In the *Ashington Colliery Magazine* for May 1940, it was reported: 'We had a visit from Bobby Main of Portia Street, Hirst, whose brother George works at Ashington Colliery. Bobby has been on a boat carrying ore from Narvik between the Norwegian ports which the Nazis recently nabbed. Bobby Main has been bombed twice and torpedoed once, and he has seen two submarines sunk by British destroyers. He says he will soon be back at Narvik again when they "get it cleaned up".'

The Kirkups were living in an upstairs flat in Poplar Street during part of the war. The back lane was always full of children. Here are a few in our backyard. They include: Elsie Berkely, Sheila Davison, Rene Davis, Billy Warburton, Phyllis Smith and Alan Harrogate.

During the war, I remember that we were asked to bring biscuits to school (St Aidan's) which were stored in a cupboard until an air raid warning sent us scurrying like scared mice into a cold damp shelter that had been erected next to the wooden Infant School buildings. To keep spirits high, the teachers started us off on a singsong. Often, after a heavy downpour, the floor of the shelter became waterlogged and we had to stand singing on the benches.

One day around 1941 someone from the council cut down all the iron railings on the Police Station wall, near the 'big' school at St Aidan's. This was a common practice throughout the country as fences were ripped up and recycled to become ammunition, although the effect of stripping England bare of railings, seemingly, was minimal.

Dozens of boys and girls ran from school that afternoon and began to play on the small strip of wall which stood about two-feet high. One by one I pushed my schoolmates off the wall, and one by one they jumped back on again, laughing and giggling at this new-found game. Except for Frankie Embleton who fell awkwardly upon the stone wall itself so that a piece of iron that had not been shaved off completely, pierced the poor lad's back. It was a hospital job and Frankie's mother, who came into school the next day, said the doctor had told her if the spike had penetrated one more inch into Frankie's back then he would have been a goner.

Frankie Embleton, 2nd left, worked as a mechanic for Jimmy Main, seen far right outside his Laburnum Terrace shop in the 1960s.

Back in the 1940 *Ashington Advertiser* notices of concerts were commonplace: 'A Weekly Concert for Soldiers' every Monday evening in the Middle Market Club with pianist Ralph Reay. The Hirst Progressive Social Club ran concerts: 'To provide Xmas Gifts for members and members' sons serving in His Majesty's Forces'. Artistes appearing on 12th December 1940 included Madam

Poxton, Peter Rigg, O'Keefe the Comedian, concert chairman was Temp Atkinson and on piano G. Thompson. The Comrades Club and the Fell 'em Doon ran Sunday Night Go-As-You-Please shows with a two pound prize featuring Tommy Camsell and Ralph Reay, respectively, on piano.

The vexed question of Sport on a Sunday was solved by Ashington Council passing by fourteen votes to six that: 'Sunday games should be allowed in the Veterans' Hut at Hirst Park.' Prior to this, the park-keeper had been struck by an old man while trying to take away his dominoes.

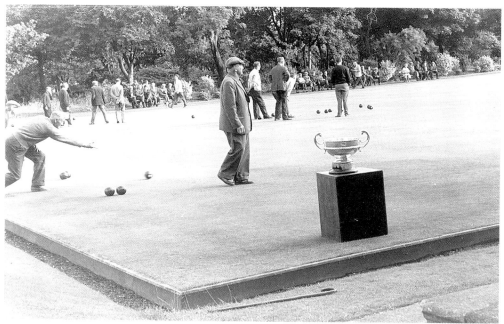

No sign of fisticuffs here as the home team of Hirst Park battle it out for the honour of winning a trophy.

It was in July 1941, when I was seven years old and living in Poplar Street, that a Saturday morning visit to the Hipp almost got me killed. When the pictures came out, my friends walked home, but, being lazy, I caught the bus at the White Elephant. The nearest stop for me was at the Garden City Villas corner with Milburn Road. I got off the single-decker bus, saw that a lot of people were waiting to get on, and decided to run across the road in front of the bus.

Unfortunately, I hadn't seen a wagon   a three-tonner belonging to Andersons the Fruiter – overtaking the stationary bus. It hit me square on, ran right over the top of me, and for a few seconds I was out cold. I regained consciousness to find the driver bent over me. I looked up, only to see the oily underbelly of the wagon. I was lying in the middle of Milburn Road, underneath a three-ton truck.

The driver asked me if I could move. I tried to get up, but my right hand was still firmly lodged under the back wheel. When he realised this, the driver jumped back into his cab and eased the wagon forward a couple of feet. By then a crowd of onlookers hustled around for a better view of the small boy with the squashed and bleeding hand. I definitely wasn't laughing after having being knocked down.

Carrying a gas mask was obligatory during the war. You can't see it, but it was in a case hanging from a strap over my shoulder when my mother and I were in Hirst Flower Park in 1940.

By the time I had reached my seventh birthday I had discarded those awful specs they made me wear to cure a 'lazy' eye. If the haircut looks spartan it's 'cos my father cut my hair right up until I was fifteen – then I went to Tommy Gallagher's barber shop beside the Mortimer.

I have recollections of being stretchered on a trolley along the corridor of what I later learned was Ashington Hospital. My mother was beside me plus a figure in white, later identified as Dr Bonar. It was he who loomed over me in the operating theatre and pressed a piece of black gauze against my mouth. Ether. I screamed for him to stop: 'Yah chokin' us,' I yelled, again and again, before the anaesthetic began to take effect.

I awoke next morning, head bruised, an aching hand swathed in bandages, and lying among crisp white sheets in a strange bed. The chap in the next bed to me smiled and said: 'Aa hope ye divvent mek as much noise when yor awake as ye dee when yor sleepin', young'un, cos ye've been screamin' blue mordor aall neet.'

Highlights of 1944

The first of January 1944 arrived in the Hirst on a washday-blues Monday. Folks didn't know it, but the end of World War Two was still eighteen months away, and even if they had been told, few would have believed it. Pessimism and optimism had merged into one, as reflected in the speech of Alderman William Cookson at a Safety Awards' ceremony to LNER motor drivers at the Grand Hotel: 'I envisage a time when the ordinary man, enjoying holidays with pay, will own a cheap car in which he can take his family into the country. I wonder whether Ashington's antiquated system of arterial roads can carry with safety the increased volume of traffic which will ensue after the exceptional developments which can be expected in the motor industry after the War.'

Entertainment that night at the Grand was provided by the Alpha String Quartet, consisting of Bill Henderson and Tom Chambers on violin, F.S. Houghton, viola, and George Webster on cello.

New Year's Day in 1944 was a full one for Sport, even though Ashington FC had pledged not to play league football until the cessation of hostilities. At the famous Powderhall meeting for professional sprinters, two local men, Ossie Sword and R.J. Hale, both won heats. Winner of the first race at Portland Park dog track was the evergreen favourite KTM with Dashing Corporal coming in a close second.

Attention was being drawn to the problem of the town's pit heaps at Ashington and Woodhorn. It was already recognised that they presented a serious health problem to the community. On 10th March the Northumberland Association of Urban Councils reported: 'The new process of delivering refuse on to Ashington pit-heaps increases the height thereof, with the result that light and breathing space is depleted. This, coupled with the smoke and fumes, is bound to have a detrimental effect on the health of the community.'

Ashington Colliery had just introduced an aerial ropeway system to carry its waste to the sprawling heap. Gangs of small boys gathered to watch, fascinated, as tiny cable-car buckets transported their unwanted cargo to the top of the festering black slope. The heaps often flared into life as the contents were strewn from above. It became a leisure-time activity for the children as the giant mountain turned into an escalating Everest on their own doorstep. Ashington Colliery's pit heaps spread all over the north of the town.

A Ronnie Patterson photo taken in the mid-1960s shows an excursion train on a visit to Ashington – see pit heaps in the distance.

On 6th March 1944 Cllr John Brotherton likened Ashington and Hirst allotment holders to 'Everybody's Cinderellas'. He was referring to two more sites of gardens that were being lost; the first because of a new extension to the

Darnley Road Mining School; and the second to make way for 120 houses at the end of Woodhorn Road, destined to become Woodhorn Villas (built in 1949). Seen here in 1951.

At Ashington Magistrates Court on 13th March 1944, W.N. Craigs, while prosecuting an Ashington man for stealing another man's tokens from a coal tub, said: 'The practice introduced last year of placing tokens on the *outside* rather than the inside of tubs, opens the way for dishonesty.' The man was accused of obtaining one shilling and tuppence to which he was not entitled. He was fined £5 plus costs. This Humphrey Spender photo shows token lads on Woodhorn Heapstead around 1938. You can see the tokens hanging on right-handle of first tub. The hut on right with 'No Admittance' on door was the checkweighman's cabin.

The Ashington Sea Cadet Corps celebrated its first birthday in April 1944 with a Parents' Day at the Princess Ballroom whose owner, Alf Shepherd, was chairman of the management committee of the Corps. Mr Shepherd presented the cadets with six sets of drums, while bugles, donated by James Chrisp and other local businessmen, were accepted by commanding officer, Lt D. Sutherland. That presentation proved to be one of the last functions held at the ill-fated Princess Ballroom as three days later it was burned to the ground on 'all-the-fours': the 4th April 1944. Officers on front of photo included schoolteacher Jack Cairns, Lieut Sutherland the CO, and bandleader Harry Hogarth. Spot cadets Harry Crowe and his mate Vince Jarvis in centre of picture.

All that was left of the Princess Ballroom was a tangled mass of steel.

Professional running got under way in July 1944, and two Newcastle United forwards, Charlie Woolett and Jackie Milburn, entered the £40 80-yard handicap at Croft Park, Blyth. Neither footballer managed to trouble the judge, but four Hirst runners: Norman Anderson, Norman Main, Cliff Campbell and W. Johns (boy) won their heats. Cliff Campbell, running under Cliff of Ashington, went on to win the final. The following week another Hirst sprinter Nichol Dalkin, running as J. Nichol, won the Blyth final.

I remember vividly my first ever visit to the ill-fated Princess Ballroom. The family were then living in Poplar Street in an upstairs flat above the Berkelys. Around 1941, Tommy Berkely and his maraa Ed Davis decided to go to the Rink, as we knew it, for an afternoon's session of roller skating. They invited me along, or maybe my mother pushed them into it – she liked to palm me off.

I was only about seven at the time and much smaller than the other two older boys. We made our way around the back of the Wallaw Cinema, behind Donkin's bakery and down a cobbled street. The Princess was nothing to look at from the outside, but once you entered those double doors it was as if you were going into Aladdin's cave – there were bright lights everywhere.

Having paid our sixpence at the door, we joined a long queue of other youngsters – it must have been during the school holidays. When we got to the counter, a man dishing out the skates asked what size we took. Tom and Ed gave their sizes, but I only took a small size at that age and was told that they didn't have a pair left that would fit me.

I literally choked back tears as I watched the two other boys fastening on their skates and hobbling out on to the rink. I leaned on a rail watching dozens of kids skating around the magnificent parquet floor, feeling as miserable as could be.

Most skaters just whizzed around the floor, but the more adept at the sport danced to canned music played through loudspeakers on the stage. Suddenly, the records were switched off and out of the throng of skaters came a slim figure, dancing majestically on skates, but at the same time playing a violin. I found out later it was Billy Mason who had once been the youngest member of Dryden Phillipson's resident band. Billy was playing, what else, but the *Skaters' Waltz*.

This is the Ashington Rink roller skating team who, according to a *Journal* headline, were 'Champions of the North' in the late 1920s. Back row: Alf Shepherd (the Rink's manager), Frank Oxberry, W. Parker, A. Cairns and Jack Allen who later managed the Regal Cinema. Front row: Fred Davison, Matt Robson and F. Harding. The poster on right says they were playing South Shields Spa that week – the Rink team won by 7-0.

Hirst folks were well used to queuing for food as the war dragged on into its sixth year, but it was waiting of a different sort which was queried by an Ashington councillor in 1944 following complaints that the cinema queues at the Regal were getting out of hand. It was suggested that the management (Walter Lawson) bring back the system of booking seats in advance which had worked so well in the past. Another councillor remarked: 'No Ashington housewife wants to spend all day working in the kitchen, then, just when she should be putting her feet up, be asked to spend up to an hour standing in this time-wasting exercise.'

Above: Walter Lawson, seen in centre with his second wife Jean, owned all the cinemas for miles around. Here he treats his staff to a Christmas Party at the Trade Union Hall in early 1950s.

Left: When the Wallaw Cinema closed down on 2nd August 1982, there was much sadness in Hirst Ashington. It was the end of an era – the last of five cinemas to close. Now, in 2003, only the Piv remains, albeit as a bingo hall. Seen here on the last day with the Wallaw staff is projectionist Denis Cleugh (hands on hips) and Jean Herron the cinema's last manager, in foreground.

Pitwork could be every bit as dangerous as fighting in the front line. This was borne out when 16-year-old Ronald Easydorchick of 194 Maple Street, a haulage hand at Ashington Colliery, was killed in 1940. One man who survived to draw his pension in 1940 was Dan Mackenzie of 52 Ariel Street, Hirst, who had been working at Ashington Colliery as a hewer, filler and shifter.

As a youth I was always mad keen on running. This is me getting the RAF team off to a good start in the relay at RAF Goch in Germany in 1958. It was a familiar sight to see racing 'around the block' taking place in Pont Street and Milburn Road, separated by a back alley, the bin corners and netties, a distance of about two-hundred yards. Each race was a handicap, sometimes organised by old Geordie Poole (who was probably only in his fifties then, but to us young'uns everyone over twenty-five qualified as being 'old'). Another fella who befriended us kids was Bob Miller. In the mid 1940s Bob was man of about thirty, dark, swarthy and lean. He had been a bit of a boxer, but most of all he was a professional runner – and a good one.

Bob Miller was one of the region's best when it came to sprinting. Many said he should have won the gold medal at Powderhall the year that Dusty Down won in 1947. But it wasn't to be, and Bob ended his days on his own living next to my parents at 185 Chestnut Street.

And talking of Dusty Down – he is seen here (2nd right) with his brothers and his father behind the bar at the old Northern Club on Woodhorn Road where George (Dusty) was steward for a number of years.

Another great all-round sportsman was Edwin Poxton who had the honour of winning a gold medal for sprinting and for winning the half mile a few years later. Eddie ran as F. Loss, named after his dog, Floss.

Professional running was to play a big part in my life in my late teens. But for now I was only a schoolboy, and a wayward one at that. It wasn't just lads who raced around the block at Pont Street in the immediate post-war days. Across the back alley at No 82 Milburn Road lived Betty Cain, sister of Bill and Joe.

And Betty was one of the fastest girls I had ever come up against – there wasn't a lad in the street could get near her. Normally we boys played street games, such as tinny or cannon, to the exclusion of lasses. All except one, and that was a thin, dark-haired girl called Annie Miller. She was a real Annie Oakley character and your original tomboy who could scale any wall, climb any rope, and hold her own against the most robust of males in any scrap or skirmish.

Betty Cain is featured left as bridesmaid at Ellen Taylor's St Aidan's Church marriage to Ronnie Mercel in early 1950s.

Towards the end of the war there was a loosening of restrictions and the brick shelters came down in the school yards along with the blackout curtains. My father had sunk an Anderson shelter deep down into his allotment which stood with a scores of others next to the old Ashington Hospital (seen in photo). The shelter filled up with water each time it rained, but it still provided a good hidey-hole for me and the Pont Street gang if we were trying to evade those toffee-nosed kids from 'high' Ashington. The hospital finally closed in April 2003.

Hospital and Infirmary, Ashington.

The Hirst Park became an ideal venue for sporting events. This is part of an article in the *Ashington Advertiser* of 23rd July 1949:

'Outside attractions during the early part of the afternoon included a very good gymnastic display by Sam Morgan's Ashington Welfare Athletic Team. This was followed by a comic football match which caused endless amusement, and then a fancy dress competition for children. This was won by Sylvia Finlay of 36 Seventh Row, Ashington, who was dressed as a scarecrow. Second prize went

to Enid Tynemouth of 39 Seventh Row, dressed as a Hawaiian girl. Third prize was divided between Mavis Hart and Leonora King of 21 Mitford Drive.

'The footrunning handicap, as always, attracted its quota of spectators and the event was won by J. Wendell (Joe Wilkinson) of Choppington. (Seen lunging for the tape, far left, in the final.) General secretarial arrangements for the Show were carried out by Mr J. Grieve of 21 Sixth Row, Ashington. The industrial section with its wide range of exhibits denoting fine work in bakery, confectionery and needlework was won by Mrs Summers of the Second Row.

'The foot handicap was organised by Mr Tommy Lyons, assisted by his brother Charlie as starter and Mr Tommy Clough as caller. The large number of heats were witnessed by one of the biggest crowds ever seen for such an event. This

photo shows Billy Lyons (2nd left) winning his cross tie from George 'Copper' Reed (on left), R. McGowan and Alan Ventners.'

On 11th October 1954, almost on the eve of Woodhorn Colliery Band's departure to play in the finals of the National Brass Bands Championship in London, their bandleader, Archie Locker, resigned, saying: 'I am leaving because there is no co-operation between the officials and the band. Several decisions have been made without our knowledge and the general atmosphere is unsatisfactory. I will take up a position with some other band. Chopwell and Pegswood have approached me already.' Said the *Evening Chronicle*: 'Mr Locker made his last appearance with the band this weekend at a concert to raise funds for next Saturday's London trip.' Archie's brother, Jack, also a member of the band, said: 'The committee decided that the band wanted a professional conductor to conduct them in the national finals. Yet, when we took a vote at a rehearsal, 18 out of 19 were against it.' The five-year-old band was financed by weekly contributions of 3d from the Woodhorn Colliery miners. Since Mr Locker took over in 1953 the band had won seven prizes in four contests.

Woodhorn Colliery Band had a lady member in the early 1950s when young Ann Mackintosh (front centre) daughter of Police Inspector Jim Mackintosh, played the cornet. Ann later played for the famous Ivy Benson all-girls band. Other band members included: Kenny Walsh, Ernie Johnson, Jackie Summers who ran his own danceband, Jack Tully, Sid Smith who had been a United bus driver before working for the NCB on the Fodens, 'Drummer' Danny Robson and Albert Crooks.

Born in 1940, John Murray, worked for thirty-three years at Ellington Colliery, and in 2003 is now employed as an attendant at Woodhorn Colliery Museum. He recalls: 'As a young lad, I lived at No 222 Hawthorn Road, right next to Hirst Park. I was very keen on photography, and I was bought my first camera when I was ten years old. It had been purchased by my uncle, Doug Murray, at Kings Cross Railway Station in 1950 when he was coming home on leave from the Royal Navy. It was a Kodak, and Doug said that it only cost him one shilling. Very soon I began to take pictures of Hirst Park.

'Around 1953, Ashington held a Festival, probably to coincide with the Queen Elizabeth II Coronation. Many events were held in Hirst Park including a competition to find the weirdest mechanical contraption. Brother Aidan wearing a gas mask is seen in front of an 'aeroplane'.'

'And this is me in the Park, aged about fifteen, with my camera case strung over my shoulder.'

GRUELLING BUT IT WAS WORTH IT. That was the headline in the *Ashington Post* in January 1950. The words were credited to Harry Harle who, running as Short of Ashington had won the coveted gold medal at the Powderhall Stadium in Edinburgh. The report continued: 'No water to drink, no smoking for three months, no late nights and muscle massage which bruised – these were just some of the rigours of training which 28-year-old Harry Harle of 29 Sycamore Street, Hirst Ashington, had to suffer in order to win this year's Powderhall foot handicap at Edinburgh.

'Less than an hour after he had arrived at his brother Jim's house at 51 North Seaton Road, Harry told the *News Post* how he won the gold medal after only one attempt at this famous sprint. Harry said: "The greatest thing anyone has got to have to win a race like that is will-power. I am going back there

again this year to prepare for the 1951 event. I had the confidence that I was going to win. Out there on the track before the final I must have been the least disturbed of everyone there. The three month's preparation under what seemed gruelling conditions at first, were worth it. Settle down, accept the rigours of training and have a strong will – that is my advice."

'Harry plans to take a fortnight's rest before going back to his painting and decorating job and then he will get in touch with his club Alnwick FC for a game as soon as possible. He is to visit his brother Jim, also a fine footballer and sprinter, who went into Ashington Hospital for an operation. But Harry won't be out on Hirst Welfare ground training on Sunday morning. "I think I deserve a lie-in," he said.'

Harry, seated, with his brother Jim.

Note: Sadly, Harry's brother Jim Harle died after an operation in hospital, soon after the above report.

Harry Harle was a hot favourite to win this final. As you can see he won it with ease.

Second Hirst Scouts were rehearsing for their own Gang Show in March 1950 at the Central Hall. The Gang included: R. Armstrong, E. Arkle, G. Buttle, A. Blair, B. Blackburn, R. Brotherton, T. Birchall, N. Crooks, B. Critchlow, G. Charlton, P. Carlton, J. Dixon, A. Davison, G. Duffy, A. Duffy, G. Fulton, F. Fenwick, A. Hunt, J. Humble, A. Hunter, J. Ireland, A. Jones, J. Johnstone, E. Longstaff, D. Mordue, S. Morgan, A. Murray, B. Oxberry, T. Owens, R. Owens, G. Patterson, A.E. Potts, J.A. Potts, A. Robertson, B. Robson, P. Rickard, J. Rowell, C. Short, L. Short, R. Sankey, M. Scott, Alex Scott, Alf Scott, A. Smith, L. Sanderson, G. Thompson, L. Thompson, George Tomlinson, L. Thompson, J. Towler, B. Underhill, K. Wharrier, A. Wilkinson, T. York, H. Yates. Producers were Arthur Potts and G.R. Anderson.

At their headquarters in a church hall behind North Seaton Road, the 4th Ashington Scout and Cub Troop had a distinguished footballer in their presence when young Robert Charlton became a member just after war. He is seen here, wearing a cap, arms folded, 5th right in the second back row. Back row: Alan Duff, Eddie Perkins, Colin Greenwood, Girling Jamieson, Jim Woods, Don Foster. Second back row includes: Bill Kindley, Reg Davies, Alan Lavelle, Harry Dodd, Micky Cummings, Bobby Charlton. Second front row includes: Jackie Scott with banner, Colin Woodward, George McPherson, John Crawford, Matty Bullimore, Ken Millican, Straughan, Stan Griffiths. Front row: George Ferguson, Hedley Watson, Stan Davis, Ed Crouth, scoutmaster John Potts, Isa Tomlinson, scoutmaster Jim Tomlinson, Derek Parmley, Bruce Parkin and George Warham.

'WOMEN FOOTBALLERS HAVE NO GROUND TO PLAY ON' was the headline in the *Ashington Advertiser* of July 1951. It reported: 'Ashington women's football team which in its first year won a cup final by nine goals to one, has no home ground to play on. "It is tough going being a member of a women's football team," said manager Jack Simmons who has been trying to get a ground for his all-conquering team for months. Now he has appealed to the local authority for assistance with a team which, he claims, will attract gates of 5,000 to benefit charity in the district. At last night's meeting of Ashington Urban Council, however, chairman of the Parks Committee, Councillor Mick Bell, spoke strongly against allowing the team to use the recently-renovated Portland Park. He warned: "We are not open to stunts."'

Jackie Milburn with Ashington Ladies football team at Hirst Park in 1951.

(Note – Ashington FC had owned Portland Park since the freehold had been passed on to them by the original owner of the land, the Duke of Portland. But in the 1950s, desperately short of cash, the directors of Ashington FC sold the ground to the local authority for £9,000, a mere fraction of what it was worth.)

The Olympic Games taking place in 1952 at Helsinki did not include a wheelbarrow race, but that event stirred up a lot of interest during the miners' holidays in Ashington in June 1952. The event had become something of an annual romp for two miners A. Bushby and J. Wood, but this time they faced intense competition from Hirst youngsters Ray McGee and Ken Key. Five barrows lined up for the one and a quarter mile race along the Main Street, but the steep incline of Station Bank sorted out the weaklings and it was soon a duel between the old timers and the young pretenders. At the Grand Corner each pair had to comply with the road sign 'Halt at Major Road Ahead'. Spectators who lined the road cheered on their particular favourites. From being thirty yards behind at the half-way stage, Bushby and Wood put on a last-minute spurt to come home victors by twenty yards. Two other pairs of contestants had thrown away their barrows and crossed the winning line aboard a lorry. Meanwhile the Ashington miners' holiday week continued with a soapbox derby and a picnic at Woodhorn Mill.

Winners of the wheelbarrow race, Alan Bushby and Mr J. Wood are seen here being interviewed by Alan Clark, a BBC sports commentator. On the left are Hazel Slowey and her bus-driver dad; in the rear is Jimmy Slowey. Towards the right are Bob Kennedy and one of the Weddle twins.

After the Second World War, one of the finest professional sprinters to come from the Hirst was Jack Thompson of Katherine Street. Running as Berwick of Ashington, he won many sprint finals including the Morpeth Olympic Games. So it came as a shock to learn on 15th September 1953 that he had been injured in a motor cycling accident when the bike he was riding hit a lamp post at the Woodhorn Colliery corner. A passenger on the pillion seat, Henry McLaughlin of Ariel Street, was allowed to go home after treatment at Ashington Hospital. Jack Thompson was taken to Newcastle's RVI where, sadly, he died shortly afterwards at the age of twenty-three.

A young Jack Thompson is seen on left in the early 1940s with Joe Wilkinson who won the Hirst Park sprint in 1949 running as Wendell of Choppington.

I shall end this volume that looks at Hirst, Ashington, with another football story: the astonishing record of Laburnum Terrace as reported in the *Newcastle Journal*:

It was a bright Spring evening in May 1967. The sound of Ashington Colliery brass band playing at Portland Park football ground carried over into Laburnum Terrace, about a quarter of a mile away. Laburnum is a street of about 25 red-brick houses built in 1897 by W.G. Gordon of Stakeford for the Ashington Coal Company and costing £93-10s-0d. The back doors are really front doors, opening on to a concrete-surfaced back lane, which was then both thoroughfare and communal backyard.

In the 1960s, Laburnum was occupied by mostly retired people. The houses when first built were described as 'four-roomed cottages' with two rooms downstairs and two up, designed for miners with larger families. During the Second World War, each household had an average of two young sons, and since, in Hirst Ashington, boyhood and football were almost inseparable, this meant about 50 soccer fans and aspiring players kicking a ball around the street from the moment they could walk. As seen here in 1967.

Among them were the two Charlton lads, Bobby and Jackie, from No 18, and young Jimmy Adamson from No 31. Cissie Charlton often said that the greatest footballers were born not made. But the same streak of lightning which endows football players must have struck the same place, not twice, but three times. For on Thursday 14th May 1967, Jack Charlton, the Leeds United and England centre-half was to receive the title of 'Footballer of the Year' from the Football Writers' Association. By doing so he was following in the footsteps of his younger brother, 'Wor Kid', and of Jimmy Adamson to form a neighbourly triple crown of winners of one of the game's most coveted personal awards, making Laburnum Terrace the most famous soccer nursery street in Britain.

'Oh, aye, even the lasses play football here,' said Laurence Robinson a sixty-year-old (in 1967) miner. 'The majority of the men used to take an active interest in the game, but a lot of them are gettin' on a bit noo. Us fellas would often have a game in the backstreet and join in with the young lads. The polis didn't like us playin' here though, and there was always the fear of gettin' caught. Although Aa have never heard of anybody bein' prosecuted. Just to be on the safe side, like, we used to run when we heard him comin'. I encouraged me own son Laurence to play football and told him to get his toes stuck in. He used to play in the same side as Bobby Charlton in 1949 at Hirst North School. I suggested he should get on the forward-line, but he said he didn't fancy it. Eventually he just dropped oot of the game.'

By 1967, Jack Waldock had lived in Laburnum for 35 years. He said: 'The kiddies still play football in the street, and people still complain aboot the noise and the danger of havin' their windows put oot. Me youngest son, Cliff, now aged 34, and a blacksmith by trade, was given the chance of playin' professional for Whitley Bay, but he turned it down cos he thought at the time that playin' football for a livin' was ower insecure. When Aa was a laddie, those who could afford football boots paid a tanner a week into a club until they had raised the necessary ten shillings and sixpence to buy a pair. Them that couldn't afford the money torned oot in their stockin' feet.'

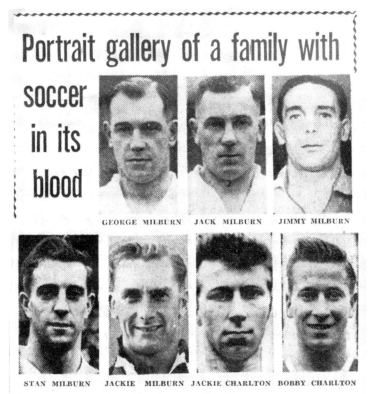

Portrait gallery of a family with soccer in its blood

GEORGE MILBURN   JACK MILBURN   JIMMY MILBURN

STAN MILBURN   JACKIE MILBURN   JACKIE CHARLTON   BOBBY CHARLTON

Mrs Jean Parmley was aged 66 when she told a *Journal* reporter: 'I have four sons, three of whom played for schoolboy teams: Jackie, Chris and Derek who was in the same Bedlington Grammar school team as Bobby Charlton. They used to practise shooty-in using the toilet door for one goal post and the coal shed for the other. They have taken the old ash pits (bin corners) away now.'

And with the removal of the ash-tips and the up-dating of the primitive sanitary conditions, this seems a good place to end a book that has looked at how Hirst has developed over a hundred-year period. The tight-knit family communities of the Hirst backstreets have gone and open spaces that were created by knocking down some houses has merely provided more car-parking spaces. But a number of trees that survived the vandals have now matured so that now, in 2003, Sycamore, Maple and Chestnut streets really do live up to those optimistic names, chosen over a century ago.

You can see real trees now among the Hirst colliery rows that for decades were trees in name only. The saplings that were planted in the 1960s are now in full maturity. I am seen here with my mother and her friend Simone outside number 187 Chestnut Street in June 1986, and I do believe that is a tree at the top of the street.

Back cover: Ashington FC had a great FA Cup run in the early 1950s, beating Football League teams to progress through the early rounds. This squad represented the Colliers in the 1949/50 season. Dark-haired Bobby Gibson was player/manager for a time before being transferred. Bobby is seen 3rd right in back row. Also in the back row are Freddie Wort (far left) and Billy Stewart (2nd right). Players seated are: Gordon Dent, Sammy Scott, Reg Charlton, George Skeen and Ronnie Harrison who was later injured and missed most of the season. You can spot George Cave in background between Bobby Gibson and Jackie Gallon; far right is Norman West.

The People's History

To receive a catalogue of our latest titles send a large SAE to:

The People's History
Suite 1
Byron House
Seaham Grange Business Park
Seaham
County Durham
SR7 0PY